How can materials and textiles enable a more sustainable future?

As design researchers we look ahead – to a time when material needs and emotional desires will be met with more creative, less impactful choices.

When reflecting on current consumption of material goods, many talk of 'going back' to a time when we produced and used less, of reducing consumption by re-establishing old habits. But at the Textile Futures Research Centre (TFRC), we believe the answer lies in projecting forward, to a future where our materials and goods are designed, produced, consumed and disposed of in radically different ways.

Worldwide economic insecurity means that many more young design companies are employing local skills and resources. SMEs are networking to provide themselves with material streams and using shared technologies – collaborative solutions to textile production. Traditional production systems, once abandoned as uneconomic, are now being reinstated and beautiful products are now being made which complement the mass production of cheap basics. Big business is taking note of successes in this area, seeking scalable translations for competitive advantage.

TFRC's research projects seek to benefit future social systems by situating designers in the vanguard of new social, cultural, scientific and technological development, and by contributing empirical and innovative research to support sustainable, resilient design.

Based across two eminent design colleges at the University Of The Arts London (UAL) – Central Saint Martins College of Arts and Design and Chelsea – TFRC hosts a community of practice-based, design-led researchers who share a vision. Our research team is augmented by PhD researchers, postgraduate and undergraduate textiles students, all participating at one of the few specialist research centres situated at an institution with an established history of design practice and teaching, one which has shaped the thinking of generations of influential designers.

TFRC examines the future of materials and textiles through three lenses – science and technology, sustainable strategy, and well-being and social innovation. Each of these platforms is distinct yet open; many researchers move between them from project to project. We strive to understand the sustainable design landscape using these different yet interconnected perspectives.

The TFRC is a strong, vibrant and active community empowered, informed and supported by our external collaborators. We believe the ability to forge multi-disciplinary collaborations and to broker relationships across industry sectors are core skills which designers need if they are going to introduce significant changes to future patterns of living. Our researchers seek out partners accordingly.

In these pages you will hear from those with whom we have conducted collaborative research and consultancy. Whether we at the TFRC are asking the right questions, using methods which are innovative and effective and achieving desirable, meaningful and viable outcomes is key, and the way we ensure that is by translating our research into the commercial world and by collaborating with industry. For Material Futures, our first TFRC publication, we worked with trend consultants FranklinTill, which proved to be an exciting and rewarding process, enabling us to finally share TFRC's work with a wider audience.

The future of the designer hangs on an ability to intervene at all stages of a product's life cycle. An inventive and appropriate selection of materials, assimilation of processes from other industries to revise manufacture, and ambitious new business models blending services with production all drive how design can revolutionise products and engineer sustainability. This is what we do at TFRC. We test theory with action. Well-designed products can be the catalyst for social benefit, personal well-being and scientific progress. Our current researchers are creating the tools that will implement and embed the shift to a more sustainably designed world.

Rebecca Earley
TFRC Director and commissioning
editor of Material Futures

Science & Technology

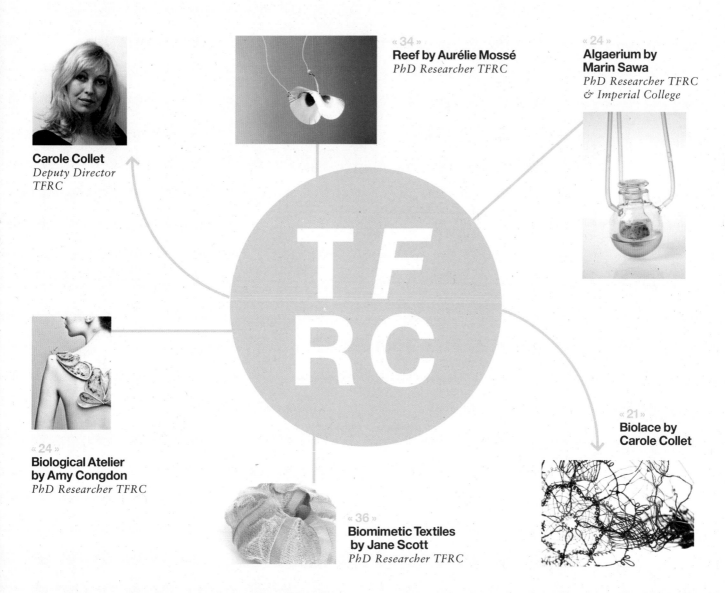

Carole Collet
*Deputy Director
TFRC*

« 34 »
Reef by Aurélie Mossé
PhD Researcher TFRC

« 24 »
**Algaerium by
Marin Sawa**
*PhD Researcher TFRC
& Imperial College*

« 24 »
**Biological Atelier
by Amy Congdon**
PhD Researcher TFRC

« 36 »
**Biomimetic Textiles
by Jane Scott**
PhD Researcher TFRC

« 21 »
**Biolace by
Carole Collet**

The Science & Technology platform investigates the potential of new technologies and emerging science fields in the context of future sustainable design. Our research work ranges from exploring past and current technologies to optimising tools, transferring knowledge across disciplines and developing high-tech sustainable design applications.

For the past five years we have also developed a strong expertise in using design research as an interface between science and design. This is reflected in various projects such as the MRC-funded Nobel Textiles Project or the TSB Harnessing Nanotechnology To Combat Climate Change project. We firmly believe that true collaborative research across science and design can lead to innovation for sustainable living.

We also project our research thinking into a far future, and our more recent focus has been on the impact of living technology on design – horizon 2050. Synthetic biology, high-performance nanomaterials and increased environmental pressures lead us to reconsider future fabrication processes. The merging of biology and nanotechnology opens up a new world where designers could well turn into alchemists. By taking the roles of curator, designer and translator, TFRC uses various research platforms to probe a far future, disseminate new knowledge and provoke new solutions.

/ Carole Collet, Lead Researcher
for Science & Technology platform

Paper Fashion by Kay Politowicz and Sandy MacLennan, photography by Aaron Til

Sustainable Strategy

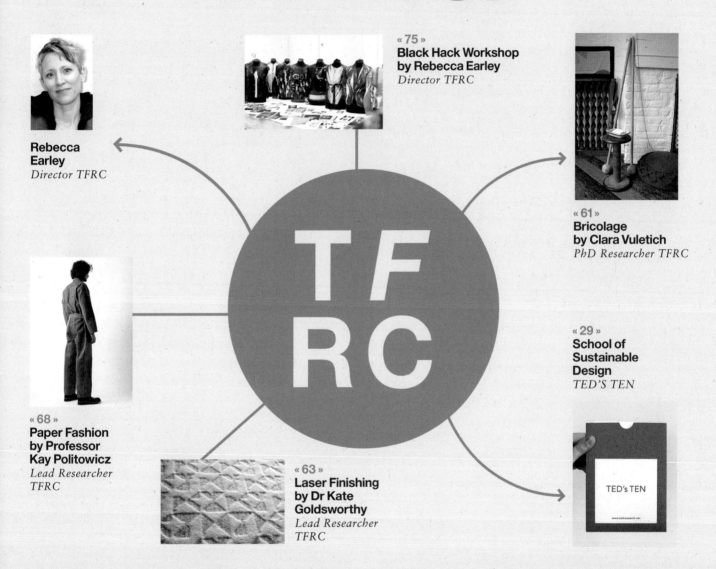

Rebecca Earley
Director TFRC

« 75 »
Black Hack Workshop by Rebecca Earley
Director TFRC

« 61 »
Bricolage by Clara Vuletich
PhD Researcher TFRC

« 68 »
Paper Fashion by Professor Kay Politowicz
Lead Researcher TFRC

« 29 »
School of Sustainable Design
TED'S TEN

« 63 »
Laser Finishing by Dr Kate Goldsworthy
Lead Researcher TFRC

TED's TEN
www.tedresearch.net

The Sustainable Strategy platform takes the notion of sustainability as a broad, holistic landscape full of potential for innovation. Of course, it is primarily about 'better' materials. But our approach is also about the design of textile systems, services and cycles which improve the flow of goods. It is about people – the people who grow, manufacture, make, sell, consume and dispose of textiles – as they are all part of the vast lifecycle of textiles. We see that it is in our power as designers to consider all of this, before we put pen to paper – or needle to thread.

With its rich experience and design-led focus, TFRC's Textiles Environment Design (TED) project aims to plug the knowledge gaps that exist in the textile industry, in the most original, provocative and enterprising ways. This involves everything from experimenting with new fibres and technologies to extending the life of textiles through design intervention and public facilitation. With the TED's TEN strategies we develop bespoke training programmes for new or experienced designers.

We imagine a textile future where sustainability is at the heart of good design and products exist in both fast and slow looped systems. We have a vision of design education and training comprising young and experienced designers and businesses from SMEs to large corporations, where designers instinctively know which design decisions to make for product, people and planet.

/ Rebecca Earley, Lead Researcher
for Sustainable Strategy platform

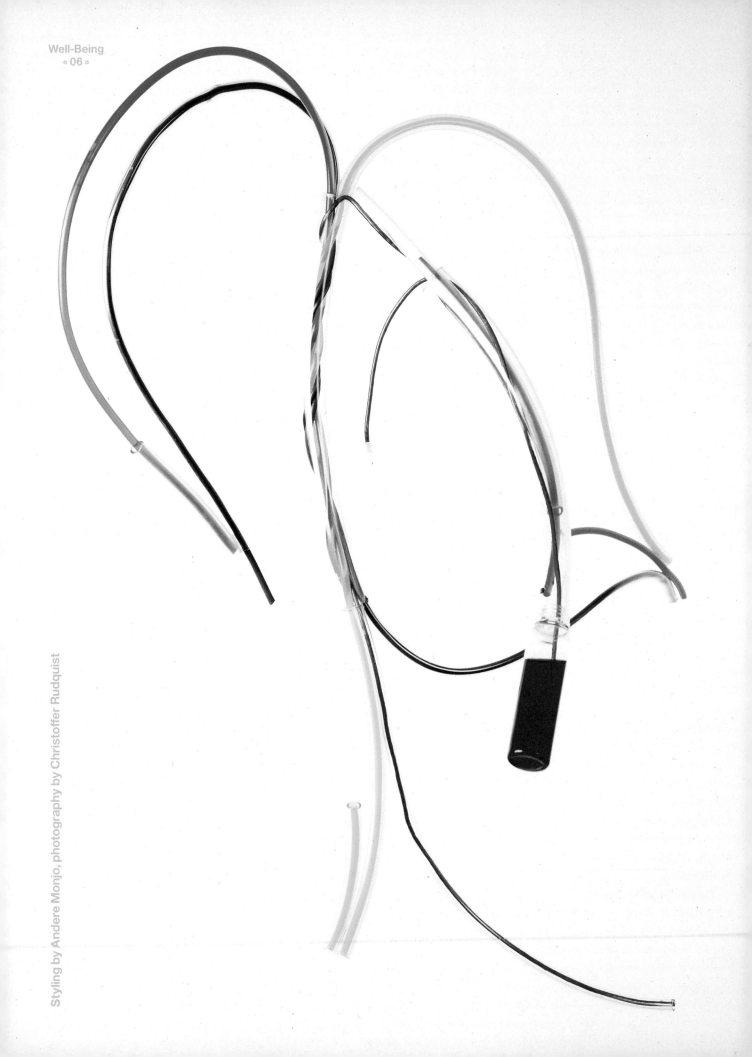

Styling by Andere Monjo, photography by Christoffer Rudquist

Well-Being

Dr Jenny Tillotson
Lead Researcher
TFRC

« 63 »
**Wandering
Methods Workshop
by Linda Florence**
Associate Researcher
TFRC

« 53 »
**Scentsory Design ®
by Dr Jenny Tillotson**

« 56 »
**The Transformative
Chronotype by
Julie Yonehara**
Graduate MA
Textile Futures

« 63 »
**Threads and Yarns
Workshop at the
V&A organised
by Jo Morrison
& Anne Marr**
Associate Researcher
TFRC

« 83 »
**Daily Poetry by
Ingrid Hulskamp**
Graduate MA
Textile Futures

« 65 »
**Taking Time by
Linda Florence**
Associate Researcher
TFRC

The TFRC Well-Being platform explores the ways in which designers can instigate social change and improve health and well-being. An impending epidemic of stress and depression could almost triple the risk of heart disease, so our research here has relevance to the future health of the nation. We are working with world leaders in biosensors and point-of-care diagnostics to develop new design solutions to advance well-being for the benefit of human science.

We acknowledge key agendas such as an ageing population and personalised medicine, and our research ranges from knowledge transfer to collaborations across a variety of disciplines from the life sciences, complementary medicine and neuroscience. Over the past seven years, we have successfully fused new technologies in the biomedical sciences with the ancient art of perfumery to enhance well-being. This is evident in projects such as Lift My Mind and Smell The Colour Of The Rainbow.

Our research within this platform also focuses on social innovation. We use design-led concepts in collaboration with a range of stakeholders to address a variety of issues: factories, their workers and waste; co-design and community workshop projects in emerging economies; and public health scenarios. We think ahead to the far future as pioneers of new technologies and concepts which will be utilised in all aspects of healthcare and personal well-being, including the monitoring, combating and diagnosis of chronic diseases.

/ Dr Jenny Tillotson, Lead Researcher
for Well-Being platform

Material Futures

Commissioning Editor
Rebecca Earley, Director TFRC

Associate Editor
Carole Collet, Deputy Director TFRC

Material Futures was edited, compiled and designed by FranklinTill for TFRC

FranklinTill
www.franklintill.com

Directors
Kate Franklin
Caroline Till

Senior visual researcher
Ann-Kristin Abel

Junior visual researcher
Floor Kuitert

Designer
Laura Gordon

Copy editor
Hester Lacey
M Astella Saw

Contributors
Bradley Quinn / Grant Gibson
/ Marie O'Mahony / Clara Vuletich /
Super-Collider / Christoffer Rudquist
/ Andere Monjo / Rebecca Earley
/ Sian Weston / Miriam Ribul / Rebecca
Malinson / M Astella Saw

With thanks to the following organisations for their support with this publication

H&M
www.hm.com

MISTRA Future Fashion
www.mistrafuturefashion.com

VF Corporation
www.vfc.com

TFRC
www.tfrc.org.uk

Lead Researchers
Rebecca Earley, Director TFRC / Carole
Collet, Deputy Director / Kay Politowicz /
Jenny Tillotson / Kate Goldsworthy

Associate Researchers
Melanie Bowles / Philippa Brock / Linda
Florence / Anne Marr / Jo Pierce / Caryn
Simonson / Caroline Till / Mo Tomaney

PhD Students
Matilda Aspinall / Jen Ballie / Amy
Congdon / Susan Noble / Aurélie Mossé /
Marin Sawa / Jane Scott / Clara Vuletich

Research Assistants
Miriam Ribul / Natsai Chieza

TFRC Manager
Angela Hartley

CSM Enterprise Support
Monica Hundal

RMA Support
Itamar Ferrer / Maria Hoang

TFRC Line Managers
Anne Smith / David Garcia

Printed by
Nino Druck
www.ninodruck.de

Print Consultants
Hurtwood Press

Editors' Letter

Material Futures from the Textile Futures Research Centre (TFRC) presents a dynamic landscape for the future of materials.

As a design and trend consultancy we believe it's important to contextualise emerging research and development so you can observe WHO is driving the advancements, WHY it's relevant, WHERE it can be applied, and HOW it can lead to holistic innovation benefiting people, profit margins and the planet.

In this first issue of Material Futures we present six key themes scoping now, near and far-future textile and material research. Highlights include 'Co-Creation Futures' in which we explore the current implications of open-source technologies and the widespread proliferation of social media networks, while 'Bio-Facture' discusses the further-future implications of biological fabrication processes, exploring how biology and biomimicry can inform a new approach to design. We also delve further into the activity of TFRC, highlighting collaborative projects that translate cutting-edge research to commercial design applications, working with clients such as VF Corporation, H&M and Nissan Design Europe.

Across the next 80 pages we unpack the cutting-edge research and development taking place within TFRC, as well as a run down of the most exciting design research globally, framed by emerging trend themes impacting the design industries. Contrary to the belief that trends are seasonal, we are always looking at longer-lasting movements, mapping their continuous evolution from the periphery to mainstream adoption. TFRC is working at the forefront of textile and material research and this publication aims to provide an invaluable source of information and insight for anyone working within the fields of colour, materials and design innovation.

Kate Franklin & Caroline Till

Directors of FranklinTill
and editors of Material Futures

Contents

TFRC News

**Reassemblage
Clara Vuletich**

Exhibition

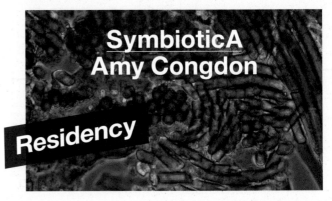

**SymbioticA
Amy Congdon**

Residency

Clara Vuletich is a member of design collective Bricolage and co-curated and exhibited her work in the Bricolage + friends exhibition at the Centre Commercial in Paris in June 2012. The Bricolage project was formed by five female textile designers who are exploring the spaces between design, craft, research, product-making and socially engaged practice. The collective believes textiles should have a long life and become modern heirlooms, and they use existing materials to create new objects and meaning. Focusing on the influence textiles has on product design and fine art, they invited key London-based designers to exhibit alongside them. The acclaimed Studio Glithero and Max Lamb were among the participating jewellery, product and furniture designers.
/ www.claravuletich.com

In July 2012, Amy Congdon was awarded a Central Saint Martins bursary to start a part-time PhD with the TFRC group. After graduating from MA Textile Futures in 2011, Amy pursued her research into tissue engineering for her project, the Biological Atelier at SymbioticA in Perth, University of Western Australia. The opportunity to work in the laboratory with scientists led her to study tissue culture techniques and to investigate the ethical implications of using life as a raw material for her design work. With this experience, Amy continues to develop her practice as a textile designer, with the aim of growing skin cells on digitally embroidered scaffolds and ultimately fully integrating textiles with the body.
/ www.amycongdon.com

**Soft Structure
Marin Sawa**

Award

Marin Sawa's Soft Structure, a unique silkscreen printing technique she developed during her MA studies in Textile Futures at Central Saint Martins, has won the Color In Design Award 2012 sponsored by Pantone. She developed the spatial geometrical pattern in the 3D virtual space of computer modelling software to print smoothly graduated colours onto fabric. This achieves a three-dimensional feel and a shimmering colour effect. Marin is now employing heat-reactive pigments to enhance her work. Soft Structure will be featured on the Pantone website later this year.
/ www.marins.co.uk

The success of the Marks & Spencer and Oxfam clothes exchange initiative, which has encouraged the donation of over 10 million items, led to the launch of Shwop Lab in East London's Old Truman Brewery. TED's PhD student Jen Ballie collaborated with the Lab and the Centre for Sustainable Fashion to organise a co-creation workshop called Unpick and Remix. Eco-conscious visitors got involved in the curation of their own fashion looks with the support of social media such as Pinterest and online mood boards, and experimented with fashion and the construction of new looks from discarded clothing. / www.jenballie.com

**Unpick
& Remix
Jen Ballie**

Workshop

Elaine Ng Yan Ling, who gained an MA in Textile Futures in 2010, has presented her Naturology design concept, which she started during her studies at CSM, in front of an audience of 600 at the Lyceum Theatre in Edinburgh and online through the TED fellowship network. Elaine is investigating biomimicry and combining nature and technology as a starting point for innovation. Her unique work led to her being invited to apply for the prestigious TED fellowship programme and she qualified as one of 19 TED fellows selected in 2012 from 1,500 applicants. Elaine now benefits from a large network of people with the same vision and work momentum, coaching support throughout the year and a dissemination platform to raise awareness about smart textiles and shape memory polymers. / **www.ted.com/fellows**

Book Launch

Melanie Bowles is launching the second edition of her book 'Digital Textile Design', published by Laurence King. In collaboration with Ceri Isaac, she has developed a guide to everything a student and practitioner should know about digital printing and designing of textiles. The new edition looks at the most up-to-date developments in Adobe Creative Suite and new work on the digital landscape. Within her practice as designer and researcher and also as senior lecturer in Digital Textiles at Chelsea College Of Art & Design, she acknowledges how the technique has changed the possibilities in textiles to open up unlimited resources and a new visual language. The book also includes instructions and acts as a comprehensive guide to current best examples of digitally printed design.

Image courtesy of Laurence King Publishing / Simon Pask

/ **www.melaniebowles.co.uk**

Digital Textile Design 2 Melanie Bowles

TED Fellowship
Elaine Ng Yan Ling

Events / Workshops

People's Print Melanie Bowles

Melanie Bowles co-founded the People's Print project with Dr Emma Neuberg to explore creativity as a tool which allows everyone to participate in the design process and to create bespoke garments for themselves. Her work lies at the intersection between handicraft and digital techniques and offers toolboxes and instructions to print and create garments confidently. Her recent workshop at the V&A celebrated The Great British Floral alongside the Chelsea Flower Show and created beautiful ready-to-print florals. Bowles and Neuberg say: 'The People's Print pioneers ways to counter the negative effects of mass consumerism, fast fashion and globalisation. It's about investing in people's innate creativity and giving them the confidence, vision and tools to create bespoke products for themselves and their communities.'
/ **www.thepeoplesprint.com**

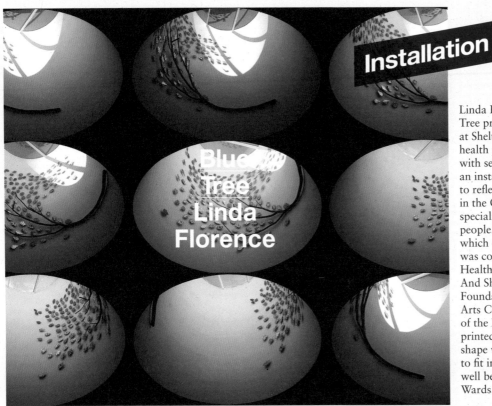

Installation

Linda Florence developed the Blue Tree project in the Redwoods Centre at Shelton, a hospital for mental health patients. A series of workshops with service users and staff led to an installation and printed patterns to reflect and improve natural light in the Caradoc Building, which specialises in services for older people. The work for this building, which opened in September 2012, was commissioned by the Arts For Health team at South Staffordshire And Shropshire Healthcare NHS Foundation Trust, with funding from Arts Council England. The leaf shapes of the Blue Tree were laser cut and printed with gold foil and the final shape was sculpted by Robin Crowley to fit into the curve of the lighting well between the Holly and Oak Wards. / **www.lindaflorence.co.uk**

Conference
3rd International Journal of Motorcycle Studies Conference Caryn Simonson

Caryn Simonson is planning a conference in association with the International Journal Of Motorcycle Studies (IJMS) and a curated exhibition to include examples of design – to include textiles, film and photography. Between 4th and 7th of July 2013 Chelsea College Of Art & Design will host the event as a collaboration between Caryn Simonson (CCAD) & Eryl Price-Davies, Imperial College London, bringing together an interdisciplinary context: Art & Design/Science And Engineering. Caryn's paper, 'Fashionable "Bikers" And Biker Fashion (exploring the fascination for the biker image and its relationship with luxury brands) was part of a fashion panel at this year's IJMS conference, University Of Colorado Springs, USA. At the 2010 conference, her paper was 'Chintz My Ride' which contextualised her photographic portrait works of fabric-customised motorcycles with their perceived 'owners'. / **www.ijms.nova.edu**

Exhibition
2D to 3D
Philippa Brock

An expert in jacquard weaving for 'on loom' finishing techniques, Philippa Brock will exhibit her key past projects and new works at the Montreal Centre For Contemporary Textiles from October to November 2012. Her solo exhibition '2D To 3D' will showcase the development from her 2008 project with Nobel laureate Sir Aaron Klug, ranging from weaves developed with Japanese paper yarn for the Warp Factor exhibition in 2009 to her most recently completed denim project in 2012. Her newest work will use smart fibres to achieve her 'on loom' method, resulting in either flat, structural dimensions within the textile or intricate 3D forms caused by different tensions between a combination of traditional and new yarns. The exhibition will be accompanied by a workshop and a paper on process-led research. / **p.brock@csm.arts.ac.uk**

Workshop

Materiality Of Light Carole Collet & Mette Ramsgard Thomsen

'The Materiality Of Light: energy-active and materially smart design for a resilient future' is an exploratory science-design workshop supported by the European Science Foundation and organised jointly by Carole Collet (TFRC) and Professor Mette Ramsgard Thomsen (CITA / Centre For Information Technology And Architecture, Royal Academy Of Fine Arts, School Of Architecture). Held in Copenhagen in September 2012, the workshop aimed at establishing the foundation for a research network for inter-disciplinary knowledge transfer between architecture, design, material science, robotics, biology, biomimicry and resilience. Scientists and designers from across Europe teamed up to establish potential joint research goals and to explore the boundaries of each others' practice, language and methodologies. This workshop is part of Carole's research goal which aims at bridging science and design to explore new paradigms for sustainable design.
/ **www.materialityoflight.org**

Book Launch

Textile Visionaries Bradley Quinn

Bradley Quinn's book 'Textile Visionaries', to be published by Laurence King in February 2013, looks at how technologised textiles and sustainable fabrics are driving new developments within the industry. The book will include works by TFRC researchers Carole Collet and Aurélie Mossé as examples that combine art, design, technology and sustainability. The book will be a relevant resource for anyone interested in contemporary textile design; each chapter will explore a theme such as technology, sustainability or innovation. Bradley Quinn is the author of other key books, including 'Techno Fashion' and 'Textile Designers At The Cutting Edge', and various articles and trend forecasts for the international fashion and design industries.
/ **www.laurenceking.com**

Lift My Mind is a technical hydration backpack designed for The North Face by Jenny Tillotson to revitalise runners. In collaboration with Ceroma Ltd, the VF Corporation commission aims to improve health and well-being using evidence that certain essential oils can influence mood, physiology, behaviour and emotional states in humans. The backpack is embedded with disposable solid scent cartridges from which scent is delivered electronically; the wearer can choose which to use to improve performance. To bring down production costs, the next stage of this aromachology project will be supported by printed electronics, but at this stage the patented Ceroma technology for the design is compatible with electronics as it does not use a liquid delivery system. Thanks to: Simple Essentials – essential oils; Joy Adams – Technician; EG Technology – Scent dispensing unit. / **www.smartsecondskin.com**

Workshop

Wandering Methods Linda Florence

Enhanced Performance Jenny Tillotson

Prototype

Wandering Methods, Linda Florence's local community project at Rathfarnham Castle, facilitated in collaboration with Maeve Clancy, involved Dublin-based participants who intended to interpret and revive the history of the castle through craft. The participants learned craft skills like paper cutting and silkscreening to respond to the shared heritage of their locality and its architectural and decorative details. These have been studied with drawings and photography and translated into individual and collective interpretations of the space. The May 2012 project was developed into an exhibition with the support of Bealtaine Festival and Craftspace (UK) in partnership with the Office Of Public Works.
/ **www.lindaflorence.co.uk**

CSM students from MA Textile Futures and MA Innovation Management entered the EDF Sustainable Design Challenge and were among the winners selected to display their Energy Diet project in the EDF Pavilion during the London Olympic Games. The project is a communication tool that challenges energy-usage behaviour in a playful way, visualising energy consumption in terms of food and movement. The project's video presentation displays equations that explain energy consumption in terms of activities and meals and the website offers a 'play' function that generates further examples, while a prototype 'pasta machine' was devised to illustrate the concept and inspire ideas around sustainability as a give-and-take equation.
/ **www.design.edf.com** / **www.energydiet.co.uk**

En Vie / Alive
Carole Collet

Welcome to the biological century, where 'living technology' will be one of the key drivers for design innovation. We are at the cusp of a biological revolution where the convergence of synthetic biology and nanotechnology will redefine everything we do. Imagine a world where bacteria and plants can be re-programmed to manufacture materials and products. TFRC's Deputy Director and Reader Carole Collet is curating the forthcoming exhibition ALIVE: Designing With Living Technology, for the Espace Foundation EDF in Paris, which will run from April to August 2013. The underlying curatorial principle is to examine whether design-led 'living technology' can lead to a new form of high-tech sustainability. 'ALIVE' will include a range of stunning exhibits that showcase how 'living technology' will revolutionise the design of architecture, interiors, textiles, fashion and even food. Method [method.com] as a Web partner for the exhibition will be designing a dynamic 'living' website to accompany the show.
/ **www.thisisalive.com**

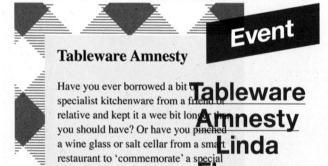

Tableware Amnesty

Event

Have you ever borrowed a bit of specialist kitchenware from a friend or relative and kept it a wee bit longer than you should have? Or have you pinched a wine glass or salt cellar from a smart restaurant to 'commemorate' a special or memorable occasion?

Tableware Amnesty
Linda Florence

Senior Lecturer on CSM's BA Textile Design course, and TFRC member Linda Florence co-organized one of the Victoria and Albert Museum's regular Friday Late events in May 2012. The Tableware Amnesty workshop invited museum visitors to tell stories about borrowed or stolen kitchenware. They were encouraged to draw the item and create a special label describing the circumstances, justifications, and any 'pay-back' required. The event, developed in partnership with Stockholm-based design group Medium, designer Tom Mower and curator Sian Weston, paid homage to cherished pieces borrowed from family or friends, and 'commemorative' souvenirs taken from restaurants. Visitors shared their stories to create an alternate narrative on material culture, and created an intriguing catalogue of non-returned items. Supported by IASPIS. **www.lindaflorence.co.uk**

Workshop

Black Hack
Rebecca Earley

The Black Hack workshop, part of the Top 100 project, aimed to deepen TED's design-led research by revaluing unwanted garments, shifting them from a user's perception of a 'bad' wardrobe item to a 'good' one. Participants made their own B.Earley shirts, drawing upon both the experience of the TFRC design researchers and questions from the non-designers. Rebecca Earley demonstrated how to create a print design on a white polyester shirt from a charity shop, using a 'heat photogram' transfer printing technique. 'The large majority of fashion consumers have limited or no knowledge of how the things they buy and wear are made – participating in this workshop gives a glimpse of this process and perhaps an increased awareness and appreciation of the individual pieces,' says Kirsti Reitan Andersen, a TED / Copenhagen Business School PhD student. **www.upcyclingtextiles.net** / **www.beckyearley.com**

Bio-

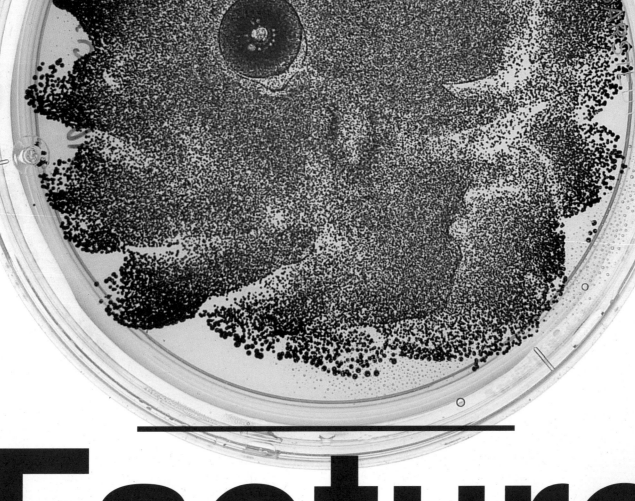

Facture

Biofacture

New textile techniques weave biotechnology, tissue engineering and borrowed-from-nature living systems into cloth. Bradley Quinn explores the biologically manufactured future of sustainable textiles

For scientists and designers, the challenge of creating new life forms is as exciting as it is terrifying. The processes and materials required to synthesise the genesis, reproduction and growth of new organisms bring risks and uncertainties – and pose questions regarding ethics and environmental consequences. As practitioners in the life sciences face these concerns, designers are also beginning to consider the consequences of changing the nature of life as we know it

Hybrid Life

The use of living systems to develop products is already evident in agriculture, pharmaceuticals and food production, where the fields of biotech, genetic engineering and synthetic biology modify living organisms to create plant cultivars and selectively manipulate animal cell cultures. Practitioners in these fields recognise the potential to create hybrid life forms – such as bacteria-resistant dairy products that stay fresh for longer, and vegetable proteins that grow synthetic 'meat' – specifically to provide for human needs. Proponents of fields such as biomimicry, a branch of science that uses technology to imitate processes that occur naturally in living organisms, claim that syncing human design with nature's know-how will make manufacturing more efficient. Researchers in synthetic biology go a step further to engineer completely new biological parts, devices and systems, and manipulate natural processes to better adapt them for human use.

Just as the synergy between technology and biology expands horizons for science, it also takes textile design to the cutting edge. The manipulation of lactose proteins, bacteria cultures and biopolymers may make it possible to biosynthesise spider silk, while the bioluminescence of insects such as the firefly, which secretes chemicals in order to emit light, can be reproduced in fabrics that light up. The success of synthetic sharkskin as a material for diving suits has enabled athletes to set new records, while the pine cone's ability to absorb moisture through its shell and release it when opening its scales has inspired new types of sportswear and winter clothing.

When American biomimicry expert Janine Benyus studied the sensory systems of insects and arthropods, which detect pressure changes and identify a range of vibrations, she discovered a means of making clothing that can guide the wearer through the dark. Benyus also sees the potential to develop systems that emit biosonar signals similar to the echolocation used by dolphins and bats to create anticollision devices for bicycles and cars.

In Britain, interactive designer Daisy Ginsberg claims that harvesting one organism's DNA code and introducing it to the living system of another may create new models of sustainability. Techniques and methodologies developed within synthetic biology could be used to manipulate DNA, triggering chemical and structural changes within biologically based products that evolve. Materials that self repair, objects that self assemble and products that kill pathogens are predicted to emerge as a result. Ginsberg reports that researchers are already engineering bacteria to secrete keratin for vacuum cleaner casings, and can fill photocopier toner cartridges with photosensitive E. coli that perform better than ink.

1 Xylinum stool by Jannis Hülsen is constructed by draping 'grown' bacterial cellulose material over a wooden frame
2 For the project 'Growing consumer goods' IDEO have teamed up with scientists to exploit known properties of microorganisms to 'grow' everyday products
3 The Kernals Of Chimaera, by Stefan Schwabe is a microfactory producing and harvesting bacterial cellulose

1/2 *Biolace & Strawberry Lace by Carole Collet explore the potential to manufacture biologically by genetically manipulating morphogenesis in plant systems at a cellular level* 3 *The Patient Gardener by Visiondivision explores the manipulation of plants and trees to grow buildings. The two-floor study retreat will be shaped from a circle of ten Japanese cherry trees that will be bent, pruned and woven as they grow*

"The techniques practised by textile designers provide a perfect template for how scientists want to design in the future" <u>Carole Collet</u>

Sustainable Biofacture

Against this background, Carole Collet, Reader in Textile Futures at the University Of The Arts, London, and founder of the Textile Futures postgraduate degree course at Central Saint Martins College, is taking her interdisciplinary approach to textiles a step further. Collet signposted the way forward for textiles when she aligned the discipline with new paradigms of design, and refuted the notion that static structures should constitute the basis of fabric forms. By exploring sustainable principles through the lens of technology, Collet has re-evaluated the roles that shape-shifting materials, programmable surfaces and technological interfaces can play in everyday design. Collet is currently researching how synthetic biology could enable us to sustainably biofacture everyday objects in the decades ahead. Although the disciplines of textile design and synthetic biology may initially appear to be dramatically diverse, there are threads that bind. Each discipline centres on creating organised structures, and uses computer modelling as a means to develop and manufacture products. The use of fibres, organic substrates and symbiotic forms is common to both. Textile researchers study the morphogenesis of natural fibres, investigating animal microbiology and plant cell growth. Likewise, synthetic biologists analyse cell growth and monitor genetic activity across living plant tissues to understand how DNA can be modified and assembled to create sustainable products, and even make existing ones more environmentally friendly.

Collet regards the mutual interests that designers and scientists share as evidence that they can work together to create new models of sustainability. 'There is a tendency for textiles to be viewed solely through the lens of colours, textures and trends,' she says. 'Yet the discipline is underpinned by material research, product development and technological advances. Sustainability has always been central to my research interests. As a model for science, the techniques practised by textile designers provide a perfect template for how scientists want to design in the future.'

The sustainable model that Collet is exploring is called 'biofacture', a term she coined to represent her vision of how future products could be biologically engineered and 'grown' rather than manufactured by industrial processes. 'Biofacture is a question I am tackling to see if biological methods can be a model for future sustainable design,' she says. 'The first step is to look at how biomimicry can inform designers – how we can learn from nature's operating systems and closed-loop ecologies. It is already possible to harvest organisms such as algae and bacteria, and encourage them to form specific membranes as they continue to grow in their natural state. The next step is to investigate how synthetic biology can become a powerful tool to facilitate the imitation of life, simply by developing the capacity to create and programme customised living materials."

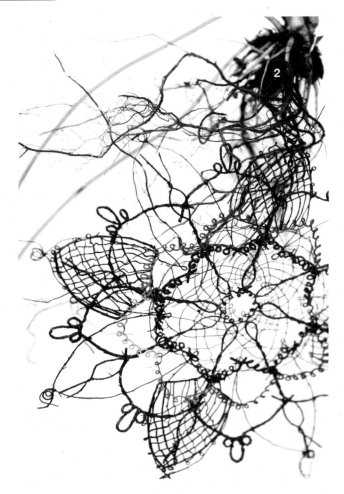

Biofacturing the everyday

Collet plans to exhibit examples of such biofactured designs as part of a spring 2013 exhibition she is curating at the Espace Fondation EDF in Paris. ALIVE: Designing With Living Technology will explore the design and biofacture of everyday products from 2050 and beyond, when, she believes, designers will be able to use biological programming tools. 'The choice of exhibits intends to address a range of concerns within the biofacture model, targeting ethical questions, such as what happens if a destructive life form is created that may threaten other habitations,' Collet says. She is reassured in the knowledge that scientific protocols require biologists to work within controlled lab experiments and use contamination-controlled environments to test the organisms they engineer, but wonders what will happen when biofacture takes place on a larger scale. 'With living technology comes a whole new set of ethical concerns,' she says. 'Biofacture also promotes the convergence of biological living matter with inert nanomaterials. For example, it is possible to attach gold nanoparticles to a sample of live DNA, thus rendering the DNA conductive. Developments like this open the doors to designing biotechnically enhanced smart textiles.'

"A hybrid strawberry plant could yield berries on its stems yet grow sections of organic lace within its roots. Both could be harvested. One would be for the food chain, the other would be for the textile industry" Carole Collet

Biofactured responses to current questions

Although much of Collet's research is rooted in the future, it also addresses some of the global issues facing design today. 'In the past two decades, we have witnessed dramatic shifts in the economics of design as the manufacturing base moved to the Far East,' she says. 'Biofacture may hold the potential to bring production facilities back to local communities and enable them to make the products they need by themselves.'

Collet further postulates that biofacture could meet the demand for luxury products, and even help prevent the spread of counterfeited goods. 'Branding could be taken to another level altogether,' she says. 'Brands could patent the bacteria and plants they use to produce textiles specifically for their products. A brand such as Chanel, for example, could potentially commission a biologically branded camellia plant that would produce Chanel tweed. If so, it would really underline the authenticity of the product by making it impossible to produce a counterfeit version.'

Planting for future purpose

By 2050, Collet believes, advancements in synthetic biology will already have had lasting impact. To that end, her Bio Lace project explores the potential to manufacture biologically by genetically manipulating morphogenesis in plant systems at a cellular level. 'I'm hypothesising how plants grown in hydroponic habitats could produce food and products at the same time,' she says. 'For example, a hybrid strawberry plant could potentially yield berries on its stems, yet grow sections of organic lace samples within its roots. Both could be harvested. One would be for the food chain, the other would be for the textile industry.'

The control and manipulation of genetic morphogenesis would enable biologists to create new and hybrid plants that perform specific functions. 'This is not speculation,' Collet says. 'There are several labs currently developing models for synthetic biology in plant systems.' The Haseloff Lab at the University Of Cambridge, where researchers are manipulating pattern formation in biological systems such as plant tissues, is of particular interest. 'The research conducted by Jim Haseloff and his colleagues indicates that it is actually possible to construct new kinds of genetic circuits that can trigger living organisms to create specific patterns as they grow,' Collet says.

Living textiles and future fashion

One of the milestones in the development of biologically engineered textiles is the collaboration between fashion designer Suzanne Lee and Dr David Hepworth, a scientist with expertise in materials. By cultivating harmless bacteria that bond active enzymes and cellulose fibres into a textile-like material, they developed a plant-based membrane that is neither genetically engineered nor created through the use of man-made derivatives.

In her BioCouture project, Lee fashions the material into prototype garments – early models of sustainable clothing designs that are ecofriendly throughout every stage of their production cycle. Lee strives to create clothing that can actually grow itself. There is potential, she believes, for biological materials grown by microorganisms to radically change all aspects of design. 'BioCouture exploits a biological material which we harvest for use as a textile,' Lee explains. 'BioCouture is not inspired by nature – it is nature.'

Another pioneer is Japanese designer Marin Sawa, whose interest in 'smart' materials has led to her interdisciplinary research degree at TFRC, working between Central Saint Martins and the Energy Futures Lab, Imperial College London. Sawa also works with microorganisms, designing and creating living surfaces derived from algae. Working in her home biology lab, she uses algal biotechnology to, as she puts it, 'explore new forms and applications of algae culture at the intersection of textile and architectural design'. Sawa uses microalgae to develop new sustainable materials, combining textile techniques with living systems. Although many biofacture models take place in scientific laboratories, Sawa's research proves that there is scope to grow and harvest materials and energy sources outside the lab.

1 *Marin Sawa's Algaerium series of algae habitats filter the air by absorbing CO2* **2** *In BioCouture, textiles are cultured in tubs of sweet green tea* **3** *BioCouture: finished product*

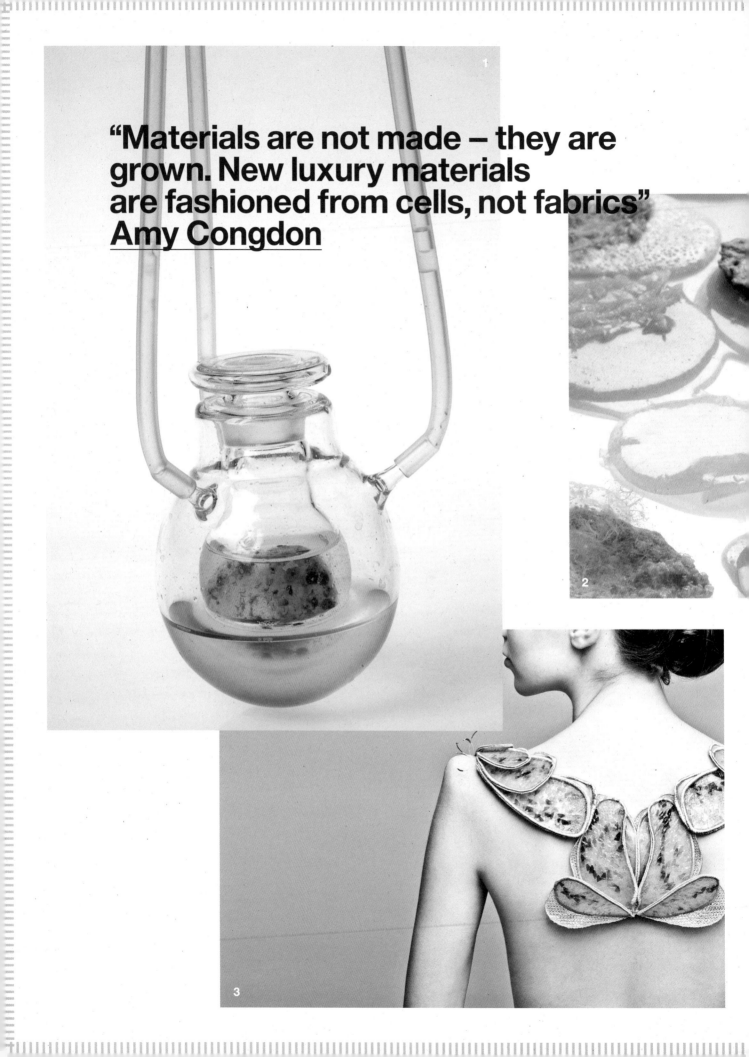

"Materials are not made – they are grown. New luxury materials are fashioned from cells, not fabrics"
Amy Congdon

Living membranes have also been developed by recent MA Textile Futures graduate Amy Congdon, a textile designer who explored tissue culture techniques during a residency at the University Of Western Australia. Collaborations with scientists enabled Congdon to explore different types of skin cells and grow them over the digitally embroidered scaffolds she had created. 'This research was not about producing finished pieces. It was about pushing my practice as a textile designer,' Congdon explains. Since then, she has embarked on 'Biological Atelier', a project that explores the design implications of the fusion of textile techniques and tissue engineering. In Congdon's imagined fashion atelier of 2080, she envisions a world where, she says, 'materials are not made – they are grown; where new luxury materials are fashioned from cells, not fabrics.'

The potential to use skin as a fashion material has inspired a range of practitioners and researchers around the world. In the Netherlands, designers Lucy McRae and Bart Hess have mooted the possibility of using genetic manipulation as a means of fashioning the future body. McRae and Hess believe that designers and scientists could collaborate to modify the textures and colours of human skin, giving mankind chameleon-like characteristics. In London, fashion designer Nancy Tilbury created prototype Flesh Dresses from materials that mimic human skin. Her conceptual work drew from her proposition that the human body may some day be capable of growing skin extensions that fold around the wearer's body to replace clothing.

Another recent MA Textile Futures graduate Zimbabwean-born designer and researcher Natsai Audrey Chieza considers the manipulation of live tissue through stem-cell technology and synthetic biology. By 2075, manufacturing is more likely to take place in laboratories than in factories, Chieza says, and stem cell biology may become 'as ubiquitous as computing'. Meanwhile, the human body will be 'genetically synthesised with home-cultured parasitic organisms' that enable it to quickly adapt to changing environments, she says. According to Chieza, there may even be potential, as genetic products evolve, for the human body to be engineered to 'farm' the materials and products it needs.

Working together for sustainability

At a time when practitioners in many fields are beginning to take nature's lead, the symbiosis between science and design promises to inspire a wider variety of visionary processes and systems than any individual discipline could develop alone. The collaborations emerging today reveal that the goals of sustainability, carbon neutrality and zero waste are coming within reach, and may one day rebalance nature and industry by making them one and the same. As new dynamics between designers and scientists continue to unfold, the synergy between them may radically redraw the boundaries of the natural world.

1 *Marin Sawa's Algaerium series of algae habitats filter the air by absorbing CO2*
2 *Design Fictions: Posthumanity in the Age of Synthetics by Natsai Audrey Chieza raises critical questions about synthetic biology and stem cell research*
3 *Biological Atelier by Amy Congdon explores the design implications of the fusion of textile techniques and tissue engineering*

[TFRC CASE STUDY]

TED'S TEN

School Of Sustainable Design

TED's TEN is a toolbox and practical resource that helps designers to address the complexity of sustainability issues and offers real ways to create and improve sustainable design. It aims to narrow the gap between thinking and doing, enabling designers to apply theory to their work in a way that is inspiring and innovative – and, above all, useful, relevant and timely

Textile Environment Design (TED) developed TED's TEN – a set of sustainable design strategies that respond to the increasingly harsh environmental impacts of the textile industry – using this disconcerting fact cited by researchers T.E. Graedel in 1995 as a basis for action. 'Eighty percent of a product's environmental and economic costs (are) committed by the final design stage before production begins' (Graedel et al, 1995:17)

TED's TEN is the brainchild of the TED research group at Chelsea College Of Art And Design, part of University Of The Arts London's Textile Futures Research Centre. TED seeks to use its practice-based research to support designers to make better choices in the design stage of their work.

Since 1996, TED has used its portfolio of international workshops and lectures to create a 'cradle to cradle' approach to sustainability in the textiles and fashion industry. Such strategies are now applied to an increasingly wide range of industries, including interiors, architecture and product design.

In 2011, the number of strategies increased in order to apply new research findings from TED workshops. These covered elements of strategic design thinking around the making, life-cycle and aesthetic issues of a product.

TED's TEN strategies function as a framework that helps both large-scale companies and small and medium-sized enterprises (SMEs) to be proactive and create real change in design and production. Through TED's TEN design-thinking workshops, the strategies can be a catalyst for companies and individuals to apply sustainable thinking to small and large-scale decisions, driving future innovation and new ways of doing business.

This approach to corporate social responsibility (CSR) and product innovation was demonstrated with a recent development of new garment prototypes for the VF Corporation in March 2012, when TED researchers and their network of key experts and designers met for FutureWear – a sustainability summit in the US where TED showcased innovative and inspiring design solutions addressing waste, fast fashion, overpackaged goods and end-of-life fabrics.

Feedback from TED workshops, including 'Designing For Better Social & Environmental Performance' at the Sustainable Fashion Academy (SFA) in Sweden, show that participants significantly expanded their skillsets when they redesigned a system around a basic T-shirt product to include service design, life-cycle thinking, and consumer engagement with new materials and better technologies.

TED workshops have made companies increasingly capable of positioning themselves within a changing market, while also addressing sustainability issues. The team has delivered tailored TED codes to companies including Puma, responding to the specific, immediate needs of their sectors while allowing them to build on all 10 strategies within larger-scale initiatives. TED codes can also be individually tailored as each role within an organisation – corporate social responsibility, marketing, production, and distribution – has a set of key responsibilities requiring a personalised approach.

TED's research team also works with individual pioneers in the industry and recently organised a workshop with upcycling brand Worn Again and scientists from Sweden and Denmark. Evaluations from designers attending the workshop said that they felt inspired and more confident about addressing sustainability within their work. The day closed with each designer being asked how they would achieve systemic change in the fashion industry. Answers included: 'Adopt an activist stance that challenges the status quo but works with business to enable new thinking... and use designers to help in that thinking – don't just use them for product!' – Nick Ryan, director, Worn Again.

*Student design outcome from TED
Workshop, Berlin 2010*

TED MANIFESTO
for Creative Innovation

This is a strategic campaign to challenge the key problems concerning the ecological responsibilities and consequences involved with enlightened design training, textile manufacture, and consumer engagement with products.

A more philosophical view is needed. Designers have been hugely undervalued in our own educational system as agents for change in relation to environmental problems.

At TED we believe it is self-evident that:

Society

should recognise
the importance of
the central role of
design to bring about
environmental change

Art & Design Educators

should encourage
awareness of the wider
context when works
are made, rather than
a problem-solving
attitude to products

Designers

should see the
importance of their
role in effecting change

Manufacturers

should be change
agents who achieve
competitive advantage
by defining value in
innovative ways

Consumers

should feel more
informed and involved
in the solutions to
a change in their
behaviour

Political Strategists

should recognise
the national business
agenda as indivisible
from a design
innovation agenda

TED'S TEN

1 Design to Minimise Waste

Design to reduce the many kinds of waste created within the textiles industry, both pre- and post-consumer, following an assessment of the impact of design decisions on the lifecycle analysis of a product

2 Design for Recycling / Upcycling

Upcycle existing garments and create them with virgin materials using an initial design process that anticipates future recycling and / or disassembly

3 Design to Reduce Chemical Impacts

Design out the use of harmful chemicals at every stage in every product's life, selecting the most appropriate material and processes

4 Design to Reduce Energy & Water Use

Design to conserve water in the production and use of textile products, including the heavy carbon footprint of consumer laundry, and consider short-life garments

5 Design that Explores Cleaner, Better Technologies

Design for new technologies to save energy and materials. Reduce environmental damage in the production of yarn and fibre, the construction of fabrics and the finishing of products

6 Design that Looks at Models from Nature & History

Seek design inspiration, information and solutions from the practices of the past and allow models from the natural world to inform the textile design and production of the future

7 Design for Ethical Production

Design to encourage, promote and maintain craft skills, locally and globally. Use design thinking to facilitate sustainable and social enterprises

8 Design to Reduce the Need to Consume

Design stuff that lasts, which people want to keep and look after, and textile products that adapt and improve with age. Also reduce shopping by substituting creative social experiences and a DIY culture

9 Design to Dematerialise and Develop Systems & Services

Develop services that are designed to support products by enouraging online / local communities of producer-consumers to lease, share and repair

10 Design Activism

Reach beyond the product to work creatively with consumers in the design of strategies to increase consumer and designer knowledge of environmental and social impacts

TED's TEN

www.tedresearch.net

TED's TEN - developed by Rebecca Earley and Kay Politowicz in 2010
– is a toolbox to provide designer-centered solutions for the reduced
environmental impact of products and systems

Sustainable Strategy Applied

TED's TEN works across a broad variety of design disciplines, including textiles, fashion, architecture, interiors, furniture, ceramics, metal and jewellery, and also within the science and business sectors. Recent clients include VF Corporation in the USA, Arup Associates, Inditex Group, Puma, PPR Home and Gucci Group in the UK.

TED's TEN has been used to underpin a variety of sophisticated events, exhibitions and publications, including 'Ever & Again', 'Top 100', 'Wall: Digital Hands', 'The People's Print', 'British-ish' and 'FutureWear'. In these projects, TED researchers have collaborated with design professionals and high-profile organisations including the V&A, the Science Museum, the Crafts Council, the Audax Textile Museum, Rhode Island School Of Design, Craftspace, and the MIT Media Lab, Boston, USA.

Testimonials

Jonathan Chapman, Puma Sustainable Design Collective

'The TED's TEN toolbox provides designers and design students with a powerful framework for unpacking the complex and often bewildering context of sustainable design. In addition to revealing a range of approaches you can take as a designer, the framework also enables you to locate yourself within the vast sustainable design debate; from this newly established location, you can prospect outwards, make your mark and become a more skilled and empowered agent of change.'

Kirsti Reitan Andersen, Copenhagen Business School

'While fashion companies increasingly realise the need to invest in Corporate Social Responsibility (CSR), TED's TEN may help them realise the potential in working with CSR. Taking the form of a bespoke design tool under continuous development – one might call it a prototype for co-creation – the 10 strategies have the potential to provide answers to the industry's call for a more adaptive and context related approach to CSR that can help understand how to identify and / or create an actionable pathway forward.'

Mike Schragger, Sustainable Fashion Academy, Stockholm

'In order for sustainable business practices to become part of the daily DNA of brands working in the fashion sector, they need to drive creativity, create energy and spur innovation. The TED team's sustainable design principles and methods are just the things to ensure this. When empowering key people in fashion companies, such as designers, product developers and buyers, with TED's tools, companies realise that working with sustainability can lead to tangible, commercially viable results, quite quickly.'

Jonas Eder-Hansen, Nordic Initiative Clean and Ethical (NICE)

'When educating the Scandinavian fashion industry in sustainability as part of the NICE project, it is crucial for us to include tools and resources. TED's TEN provides designers with hands-on examples and relevant dilemmas and have been highly valued in the NICE educational programme. Furthermore, we have been much inspired to include TED's TEN in the NICE Code of Conduct and Manual for the Fashion and Textile Industry as a concrete tool for designers to work with under the UN Global Compact umbrella.'

Respond

Repeat

Adapt

Respond, React, Adapt

Scientists, architects and designers are coming together to develop structures that respond to environmental elements and human needs. In other words the future is living, writes not-for-profit collective Super/Collider

The contemporary collision of textile design, architecture and smart technologies has prompted an evolving field of research and design where buildings, fabrics and structures become responsive and alive. We are on the cusp of a new era as the materials and structures around us change to reflect environmental conditions and other stimuli.

Driven by problems such as pollution, climate change and the need for more sustainable constructs, spaces will begin to merge with the environment around us – bringing the rhythms of nature indoors and weaving the adaptive characteristics of biological systems directly into our material world.

Living Architecture

Traditional building materials are solid and immobile, reflecting the structure they form. This is set to change as rapidly advancing material technologies push architects and designers to question the lifeless, immobile paradigm of the built world around us.

Mette Ramsgard Thomsen, an architect and key collaborator with the Textile Futures Research Centre (TFRC), worked with textile designers and engineers from Shenkar College of Engineering and Design in Israel to create Listener, a living fabric. The material is a flat CNC knit surface swirling with an irregular grid of four different fibres, each with its own structural role. These conductive fibres are knit directly into the fabric, making the material touch sensitive: the composite fabric responds to touch by inflating or deflating different segments, essentially sending air rippling below the surface of the textile, transforming it into a sea of small cocoons.

'Part of the traditional practice of textiles is to make your own materials, whereas in architecture we have always used prefabricated materials,' Thomsen explains. 'In Listener, we investigated creating surfaces that incorporate the architect's design criteria, and we explored which materials we need to invent to be able to develop a dynamic architecture. Our investigations reflect a fundamental change in thinking. Rather than imposing a static space, conceived in isolation from the surrounding environment, we can build with environmental changes, and develop something that is adaptive and changing.'

In her thermo-responsive installation, 'Bloom', Los Angeles architect Doris Sung explores exactly that adaptability. Here, a six-metre-tall 'flower' of carefully crafted metallic surfaces morphs in response to changes in atmospheric temperature or direct solar exposure. Sung uses the inherent properties of the material to increase air flow and shade as the metal 'blooms' in the heat and then retracts in cooler conditions to return to a solid, impermeable object. Such shape-memory alloys – metals that deform and then naturally return to their original shape – have proven fruitful for many adaptive structures, and have an ever-expanding portfolio of applications for designers.

Multidisciplinary practice Kinetura has developed these concepts on a much grander scale. With their project Kinetower, creative designer / architects Xaveer Claerhout and Barbara Van Biervliet propose cladding the exterior of a high-rise building with large-scale window elements. These are designed to respond to sunlight or user prompts, changing shape to regulate shade and air flow. By using a material that is rigid when taut but that becomes flexible under prescribed conditions, this metamorphosis transforms the boxy shell into a softer, undulating form.

1 *Kinetower features a responsive facade which adapts to sunlight to control light and shade inside* 2/3 *Bloom, a 6-metre tall installation has a metal skin which responds to the heat of the sun* 4 *Listener, knitted from conductive fibres, inflates or deflates when different sections of the fabric are touched*

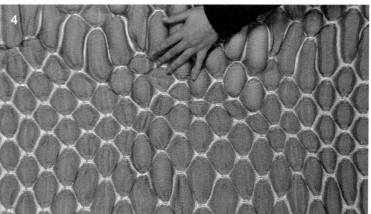

We are on the cusp of a new era as the materials and structures around us change to reflect environmental conditions and other stimuli

Design for our Future Environment

Increasing awareness of environmental issues and the need for energy efficiency drives the development of architectural elements that adapt to changing conditions in light, temperature, noise and pollution. Walls and windows are set to become responsive features as technologies move from being add-on regulatory systems, such as air conditioning, to forming integrated elements within structures themselves.

As part of the UK Technology Strategy Board's Design For Future Climate initiative, TFRC deputy director Carole Collet worked with Nanoforce scientists, Atelier Ten engineers and architects Stanton Williams to develop new design briefs for high-performance materials that could augment our ability to cope with future global warming. This collaboration led to proposals for nanocoated glass that regulates the amount of heat allowed into a building without interfering with natural light levels, as well as nano phase-change materials that can be retrofitted into buildings to create controllable heat retentive surfaces.

A similar concept informs Simon Heijdens's Shade project, in which a responsive film applied on a window creates constantly changing shadows on interior walls in response to external wind conditions. Although such shadows triggered by wind have no clear environmental advantages, the technology could be adapted to be light or temperature sensitive in environments where rapid shading is highly advantageous.

Phototropia, a project supervised by Manuel Kretzer at the Institute of Technology In Architecture in Zurich, merges electro-active polymers, screen-printed electroluminescent displays, bioplastics and thin-film solar cells to form a self-regulating installation that generates all its energy from sunlight, and responds to user presence. The project demonstrates the exciting prospect of all surfaces becoming interactive interfaces that either harvest energy from their surroundings or enhance the environment through responsive technologies.

1 *Techno Naturology by Textile Futures graduate Elaine Ng explores the intrinsic properties of natural wood in combination with shape-memory alloys to create responsive architectural surfaces.*
2/3 *Reef by Aurélie Mossé is a self-actuated ceiling installation that emulates a breathing movement activated by external wind forces, photography by Mathilde Fuzeau-Quesnel*

1/2 Hylozoic Ground by Philip Beesley is a kinetic installation moving in response to environmental stimulus. It draws in and filters moisture and organic particles from the air, is covered in sensors, microprocessors, mechanical joints and filters, and also responds to human movement

3 Manta by Guillermo Bernal, Eric Ameres, Zackery Belanger, and Seth Edwards is an interior surface that changes its form – and therefore acoustic character – in response to multimodal input including sound, stereoscopic vision, multi-touch and brainwaves

Human-Scale Interaction

Kinetic interiors that echo the constant, subtle motion of the natural world and respond to human interaction offer a poetic and engaging addition to the experience of an indoor space. As designers create more permeable, sensitive and interconnected spaces, reactive interiors come alive: they mimic the movements of nature, in opposition to other indoor spaces that stand as lifeless sets boxed off from the outside world.

'Smart technology can help a home to become a more sustainable setting – a more resilient environment,' says Aurélie Mossé, a PhD researcher investigating self-actuated materials at the Center For Information Technology And Architecture at the Royal Danish Academy Of Fine Arts, and the TFRC. Her work focuses on electro-active polymer (EAP) technologies in a domestic context. EAPs continue to be an intriguing addition to the world of materials, with varied potential uses ranging from harvesting the energy of waves to replacing muscle fibres in the human body.

A collaboration between Mossé and material scientists in Germany led to 'Reef', a hanging archipelago of sail-like petals that 'breathe' with the wind, forming a self-actuated ceiling whose elements can change shape and vibrate. 'Reef' is built upon a radically new style of actuator (a device that triggers motion) – a type of EAP known as a dielectric elastomer, which translates energy directly into mechanical work. Electricity passing through the EAP causes the material to bend. In 'Reef', passive elements of the installation are activated by gentle breathing and draughts of air indoors, while active structures are set into motion by external sensors registering the gusts of wind outside. 'These electro-active polymers could help the home to reconnect with the rhythm of nature,' Mossé explains.

Smart-materials artist / designer Elaine Ng studies the behaviour of natural elements such as wood, cane and wool in order to incorporate them into man-made materials for architecture and interior design. Her work with shape-memory materials – which 'remember' shapes in response to environmental changes – includes 'Naturology', a biomimicry project to create responsive structures and surfaces. Using 'Naturology' design, Ng created a small-scale prototype 'SAD House' made from shape-memory polymers and laser-cut wood veneer. Reacting to changes in temperature, the lace-like roof opens or closes – to increase light levels in winter or to project shadows indoors. Similarly, Ng's 'Living Furnishing Fabric' combines shape-memory polymers with the natural growth of wood grain to create a textile that responds to humidity.

Other designers are exploring how to animate interior environments from different perspectives. Perhaps the best-known example of such human-responsive design is Canadian architect Philip Beesley's 'Hylozoic Ground'. Here, a combination of sensors, microprocessors, mechanical joints and filters are intricately fitted together to form a shimmering, fairytale-like geotextile that filters moisture and organic particles from the air, all triggered by human interaction.

More recently, architects and designers at Archgeometer in collaboration with Smartgeometry created 'Manta', a ceiling-based sculpture that morphs in response to multimodal inputs – including stereoscopic vision, sound and brainwaves – in the room. In essence, the surface transforms its own acoustic character, as well as that of the space in which it is installed.

Body Responsive

Not all responsive materials need be laden with the latest digital technologies. A growing collection of designers is devising analogue techniques that use physical materials to explore the movement of the body and interact with the environment. Such projects seek to enhance the expressive qualities of what we wear, and create a stronger connection between the fabrics adorning our bodies and the environment in which we are immersed.

Dahea Sun's 'Rain Palette' is a clothing line that acts as an indicator of local air quality. The garments are coloured using a natural dye developed by Sun, which changes colour depending on the pH levels of rainwater. 'Rain Palette''s deep pinks and pale blues serve as a visual indicator of real-time environmental data – while also increasing people's awareness of the quality of their environment, and urging them to take charge of their surroundings.

In a similar vein, Tim van Cromvoirt, a designer who seeks to merge art, science and technology, has designed Thermophores, an artificial organism that completely alters the colour of its skin in response to temperature fluctuations. Although conceived as an art object, this organism could be further developed to include materials worn on the body that change colour according to external temperatures. Such materials could increase their absorption of infrared light in cold conditions and become more reflective in the heat, thus helping to regulate the temperature of the wearer.

Jane Scott, a knitted-textile design specialist currently undertaking her PhD at the TFRC, employs a low-tech approach to create bio-responsive materials inspired by the hygromorphic properties of pine cones, whose scales open and close as moisture levels change. Scott combines natural materials, including linen yarn and birch veneer, and embeds them into pockets of superfine wool, calling upon their inherent properties to concoct knitted pieces that transform from flat fabric into three-dimensional shells when it rains.

Humans have always built structures to keep the natural world outside, and dealt with the subsequent consequences as rigid constructs became aged and eroded

Future Potential

Fully responsive environments are yet to become an everyday reality, but timelines will shorten as interest and awareness build in this field. Advances are rapidly evolving, and there is understandable excitement about the potential of energy-harvesting materials that will fundamentally shift the design process. 'The whole tradition of thinking of things through a formal aspect, on white paper in the void of space, is really about the isolation of the design object,' Mette Ramsgard Thomsen concludes. 'What's very exciting about energy-harvesting materials is that they situate the environment as being central to what a design might be.'

Other influential areas of innovation are nanotechnology and the increasing use of biomimetic principles, which are driving experimentation with smart materials away from electronic-based sensors and mechanical movements towards autonomous responses – that is, 'living' systems.

Humans have always built structures to keep the natural world outside, and dealt with the subsequent consequences as our rigid constructs become aged and eroded by the elements. This outdated paradigm will change as designers and architects continue to engage with our environment in a radically inclusive manner fuelled by new developments in material technologies. With advances still very much in their initial stages, those working at the forefront of this field agree that material technologies will only reach their full potential if we create better interfaces so designers may understand how smart materials can be integrated into the environment.

This will require an increase in collaborations between science and design – making scientists aware of design criteria from the start, and encouraging designers to experiment with and critique new materials and innovations. A rapid and responsive journey from initial technological development to beneficial use in our built environment requires an ambitious and open-minded approach, one we hope to foster at the TFRC.

1 *Rain Palette by Dahea Sun utilises colour change natural dye to indicate the pH level of rainwater when the garment is worn outside. Dahea proposes the wearer scans the garment with an app when wet, uploading its acidity reading to contribute to the collation of global environmental data* 2 *Blooming Body by Textile Futures graduate Langdi Lin uses low-tech material manipulation to emphasise body movement* 3 *Thermophores by Tim van Cromvoirt is an artificial 'living' material which changes colour and shape in response to temperature change*

Inside/Outside: Burberry Design Collection

During autumn 2010, BA and MA Textile Design students at Chelsea College Of Art & Design took part in a groundbreaking design project funded by luxury fashion house Burberry

Students were challenged to examine the idea of 'value' in textiles, giving them an opportunity to take part in a live design project, showcasing fashion fabrics and environmental solutions for luxury products.

Starting with the rationale 'We cannot afford cheap things', students were asked to design a collection of fabrics using the TED's TEN sustainable design strategies as a starting point for their prototypes.

They were asked to focus their design work on long-life fabrics – which are sustainable in their continued usage and heritage quality and which also demonstrate the Burberry ethos of quality and longevity.

Christopher Bailey, Burberry's Chief Creative Officer, took personal charge of the project and spoke to students on a blog that he created specially for the project. From the outset, Bailey worked closely with each student, using their design statements to discuss their work more fully on a one-to-one basis.

He also arranged to meet the whole student group for a tour of Burberry's headquarters, to see the day-to-day creative work of an international fashion company.

Together, they explored the links between the Chelsea College Of Art & Design and Burberry. Both institutions share a deep commitment to innovation, development of high-quality design and the use of textiles. Location proved another important link, as the sites on the River Thames currently occupied by the College, Tate Britain and Burberry were once the Millbank Penitentiary – built following the principles of Jeremy Bentham's 18th-century Panopticon design. Documentation of this important historic site gave the project a strong social, anthropological and environmental detail, helping to paint a vivid picture of life in this location up to 200 years ago, including the experience of living in prison. This lent a rich source

of conceptual and aesthetic detail – imprisonment and surveillance, confinement and release, inside and outside.

Burberry provided funds for materials, processes and workshop demonstrations to fully develop the project. This allowed the Chelsea College Of Art & Design and the TED research office to put together a really exciting seminar, lecture and workshop programme, and a range of specialists who were invited to work with the students. These included Helen Carnac, a leading artist, maker, curator and academic, who led an investigation into the phenomenon of slow textiles; dress historian Juliet Ash gave a lecture on prison clothing; artist Clare Qualmann took the students on a 'darned memory' walk around the site of the former penitentiary; and textile designer Professor Zane Berzina worked with the students on intelligent fabrics, using soft technology.

The students were treated to an additional programme of craft workshop masterclasses and their experiences included explorations into coatings for knitted and woven felts with Erasmus tutor Päivi Vaarula; heat-gun applications with textile artist Dr Frances Geesin; 'drawing with thread' with textile artist Debbie Smyth; digital printing with design tutor Melanie Bowles; and fringes, tassels, pompons, cording, and knitted frills with knitwear design tutor Jane Murrow.

TED developed wood, ceramics and laser-cutting workshops, alongside a range of workshops led by graduate designers, including knotting and plaiting with Emamoke Ukeleghe; heat-press sublimation dyeing with Chetna Prajapati; crochet with Cassi Hill, and smocking and construction, led by PhD student Matilda Aspinall.

Students were encouraged to understand the techniques through example and experience and to introduce innovation into their practice through the lens of sustainability.

The rich local and 'slow' references were used to make connections between historic and contemporary construction and repair, helping students to understand the links between longevity, narrative and lasting value

The rich local and 'slow' references were used to make connections between historic and contemporary modes of construction and repair, helping students to understand the links between longevity, narrative and lasting value. There was also an exploration of local history and contemporary local design production which gave students a sense of 'terroir' more often associated with locally grown produce.

In addition, students were asked to experiment with material selection in order to express their ideas – to introduce textile techniques to develop characterful fabrics which told the 'story' of their collection, and which located and captured their intellectual concepts for making new textiles.

The sophisticated design of the Inside – Outside programme helped students arrive at some truly exciting outcomes. These included new fabric structures, surfaces and qualities, and a 'grave to cradle' perspective that gave new life to materials previously considered to be waste or of little value.

The entire process and results were captured on a project blog [http://chelseatextilestudents.blogspot.co.uk/search/label/Burberry/Project]. Here it is posssible to follow progress from initial statements and approaches, to fabric development and visual information through to final outcomes and collections, which helped to share information across the BA and MA courses and with Burberry designers.

All work submitted was reviewed by the staff team at Chelsea, including Professor Kay Politowicz, Caryn Simonson and Lorna Bircham, and also by Christopher Bailey, who awarded the Burberry Sponsor's Prize and an Internship in Burberry's studio. First prize was awarded to Mandeep Mann, second to Henry Hussey, and third prize went to Kirsty Lawson. Bailey was so impressed with the quality of the students' work that the three prize winners were awarded a total of £1,000 and an internship for each at Burberry.

1/2 *Student work by Mandeep Mann*
3 *Student work by Henry Hussey*

Co-
Creati
Future

OS Work/Shop, Brussels,
designed by LoFi-studio + Intrastructures

Co-Creation Futures

Democratic and collaborative, anti-fast fashion and pro-community generation, co-creation sees consumers sitting at the drawing board for a change. M Astella Saw explores the new maker economy

The do-it-yourself movement, reinvigorated by financial pressures and refound craft pleasures in the global economic squeeze of the last five years, has engendered a new generation of amateur makers, co-creators and prosumers. Thanks to the increasing accessibility of open-source software, digital design, rapid prototyping and other production tools, people are now able to design and produce almost anything themselves – from bikinis (Continuum Fashion's N12) to hardware components (OpenStructures) to chairs and tables (Pål Rodenius's 2440x1220 Saw, Assemble flatpack furniture).

Co-creation, or co-design, which sees regular consumers collaborating with brands and other producers to conceive new patterns, designs and products, is overturning the prescriptive, top-down nature of the fashion and textile sector as we know it. With interaction and collaboration at its heart, co-creation sees its many makers taking control.

'Co-design offers a new mode of interacting with people and materials,' says Jen Ballie, an affiliated designer at the Textile Futures Research Centre (TFRC), who is completing her PhD at Chelsea College Of Art And Design on what she calls the 'co-everything' movement. 'People have been passive consumers for so long. Co-creation is a means of regaining some form of order in a chaotic marketplace.'

The rise of the maker

We began to see shades of co-creation – hints, that is, of consumers demanding a say in the design process – in the recent trend for mass customisation. Brands including Rickshaw Bagworks, Republic Bikes and Shoes of Prey make to order, allowing their consumers to mix and match fabrics and colours to create personalised bags, bicycles and footwear.

But co-creation is about more than choosing the colour of the lining on an iPad sleeve. Co-creation is about the rise of the maker. Colette Patterns, DIY Couture and Oliver + S already cater to a new generation of trend-aware dressmakers looking to make their own lace leggings, halterneck rompers and bubble dresses. Meanwhile, modern-day makers – tinkerers,

arts and crafts enthusiasts, artists, even robotics amateurs – gather at spaces such as TechShop in the USA, which provide tools, space and expert support to people wanting to create.

Collaboration online

Co-creation is growing in popularity as the barriers to entry become ever more simple to overcome, Ballie notes. 'The web and online platforms are influencing this shift alongside the democratisation of digital design tools,' she says. 'Before, you needed a manufacturer to produce things. Now, with fab labs, MakerBots and new print bureaux, people are developing local models for design and production.'

At this year's Istanbul Design Biennial, an exhibition entitled 'Adhocracy', curated by Joseph Grima, explored a cultural and technological landscape where workshops replace factories and networks are at the heart of production. Grima argues that 'rather than the closed object, the maximum expression of design today is the process – the activation of open systems, tools that shape society by enabling self-organisation, platforms of collaboration independent of the capitalist model of competition, and empowering networks of production.'

Ballie's own Dress Up/Download workshop at the V&A Museum in London last year enabled complete amateurs, aged 3 to 83, to design textiles based on paper collages they made themselves. Using an online gallery to build a crowdsourced collection, Ballie has facilitated the creation of 450 fabric concepts to date. A small selection of them will go into production, she says.

2 Eugenia Morpurgo's Repair It Yourself project, a pair of shoes designed to be repaired, rather than thrown away, when worn out. 3/4 The OpenStructures drip coffee-maker by Jesse Howard in collaboration with Thomas Lommée 5 Makerbot Replicator 2 is a desktop 3D printer costing just over $2,000, aimed at hobbyists and professionals

Co-creation is about more than choosing the colour of the lining on an iPad sleeve. It is about the rise of the maker

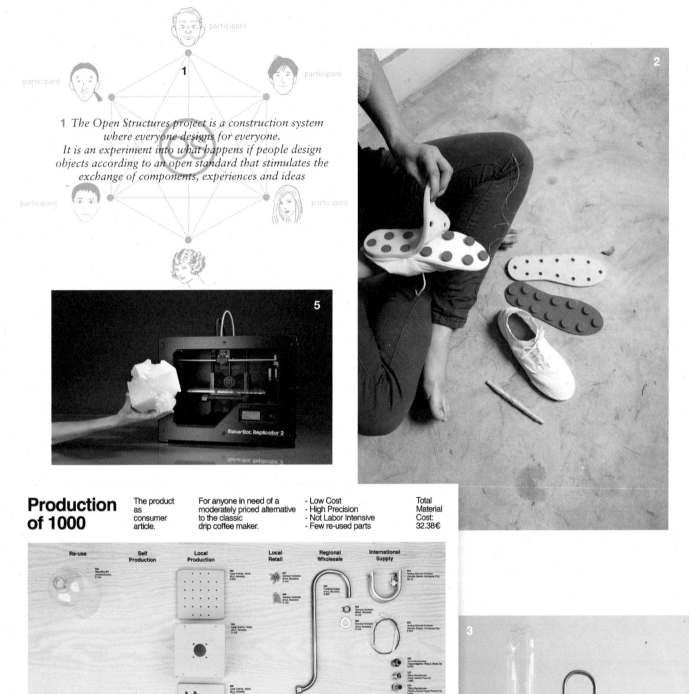

participant

participant

participant

participant

participant

1 *The Open Structures project is a construction system where everyone designs for everyone. It is an experiment into what happens if people design objects according to an open standard that stimulates the exchange of components, experiences and ideas*

Production of 1000

The product as consumer article.

For anyone in need of a moderately priced alternative to the classic drip coffee maker.

- Low Cost
- High Precision
- Not Labor Intensive
- Few re-used parts

Total Material Cost: 32.38€

| Re-use | Self Production | Local Production | Local Retail | Regional Wholesale | International Supply |

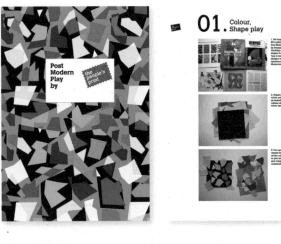

Post Modern Play by The People's Print: how to create geometric repeat patterns from cut-out pieces of paper

Co-creating, co-owning

Key to the revolution in making is people's desire to feel some sense of ownership of their work, says Melanie Bowles, a digital textile designer and co-founder of The People's Print. This is a series of workshops and e-books that seeks to pair hands-on and practical techniques with emerging technologies, thus enabling people to create their own bespoke textiles. Together with co-founder Dr Emma Neuberg, a design thinker who created the Slow Textiles Group, Bowles organised the Born To Be Wild workshop at the Victoria & Albert Museum.

Born To Be Wild saw a motley group of strangers, none of whom had any background in fashion or textiles, design and create a swatch book of original digital fabric designs for personal use. Besides producing this swatch book, the workshop also proved an ideal opportunity for the generation of a community. 'When you work in a group to co-create, you develop mini-communities to share skills,' Bowles says. '[At The Born To Be Wild workshop], I think everybody felt ownership of the work we co-created.'

The People's Print takes on a special role in providing toolboxes for consumers to design their own fabrics, and draws on Bowles's previous projects, which explored new concepts, as she says, 'for emotional, durable and sustainable design through bespoke digital print'. In her Slow Grow project, Bowles translated a woman's hobby – growing flowers – into a bespoke shirt tailored from a specially designed, digitally printed fabric showing off the sweet peas she grew.

'It's not a fast fashion thing,' Bowles says, underscoring the year-long process of creating the shirt. 'But it's got an ownership for life. Mary [the woman who grew the sweet peas] could give the print to her family to use for anything – it's their print. It's an investment that will last for years.'

Story and sustainability

Bowles's Slow Grow project and her more recent People's Print workshops also weave in an important driver of co-creation: the need for narrative. 'Co-creation is about stories – about a product's history,' Bowles says. 'There's a lot of interest in narrative.' Further, narrative is a key element of co-creation that ties in with consumer concerns about sustainability and waste reduction. By infusing a garment with a consumer's personal effort, emotion and investment – that is, a story – co-creation takes a stand against the buy-it-now-then-toss-it-out call of anonymous fast fashion.

Italian designer Eugenia Morpurgo's Repair It Yourself project consists of a pair of shoes designed to be repaired, rather than thrown away, when worn out. Mechanical fastenings on the bottoms mean the soles can be easily replaced; an accompanying repair kit includes needles, thread and fabric. The project, Morpurgo has said, puts into consumers' hands the otherwise-disappearing tools and knowledge for repairing. It also enables wearers of the shoes to sew in the unique story of their use.

Upcycling, too – transforming old clothes into new items – adds a new layer of story to a pre-loved item. In collaboration with retailer Marks & Spencer and the London College Of Fashion's Centre For Sustainable Fashion, Ballie hosted Unpick And Remix, a workshop to which members of the public brought in unwanted items of clothing to be taken apart and reconstructed into new garments. Social websites Pinterest and Storify were used to organise mood boards, tweets and ideas, while fashion students helped participants with techniques such as draping and smocking. While the fashion laboratory was well planned in advance to provide all the necessary tools and support, the session, Ballie says, was ultimately 'a serendipitous process informed and inspired by the participants'.

Before, you needed a manufacturer to produce things. Now, people are developing local models for design and production

*Unpick and Remix: where unwanted items
of clothing were taken apart and
made into new garments*

Co-creation challenges

'The nascent Maker movement offers a path to reboot manufacturing,' writes Chris Anderson in his book 'Makers: The New Industrial Revolution', 'by creating a new kind of manufacturing economy, one shaped more like the web itself: bottom-up, broadly distributed and highly entrepreneurial.'

Indeed, proponents of co-creation are creating a new kind of economy. They are demanding more of a say in how their goods look, in how they were made and where they were made. As more brands build in toolboxes for user-generated custom design, consumers keen on taking part in the design and production process may come to see retailers as enablers rather than pure producers, and will require more openness from fashion brands, especially, than they have traditionally offered.

Brands, meanwhile, will have a new challenge at hand: ensuring that they are able to retain their key brand values while sharing the drawing board with their consumers.

'The role of the designer will be crucial,' Ballie says. 'Designers might facilitate [others' designs], but they are also key to ensuring that quality and craft don't become lost in translation.'

One solution will be for brands to facilitate a hand-holding approach to co-creation. In her work for a major US retailer of streetwear, which she declines to name, Bowles consciously 'engineered' a co-creation platform defined by certain criteria, such as the look and feel of the brand. 'I knew what the brand wanted, and what the consumer expects from the brand,' she says. 'I was in tune with both.'

Elsewhere, brands and other players in the textile and fashion industry may find that they have an increasing role in providing expert support to co-creators or local workshop space where consumers eager to co-create can meet and work. 'There are very few options or services for repairing, maintaining, adapting or creating clothing or textiles,' Ballie says. 'We need service design to develop new experiences. Maybe more fashion labs, hubs and bureaux might emerge.'

Ultimately, the wealth of ideas and energy from an engaged consumer base has given the co-creation movement its momentum. Active participation from industry will help form a community richer in interest, skills and involvement – and will help weave the new fabric of our shared lives.

VF Corporation

Creating Next-Generation Apparel

Towards a new era of more innovative, sustainable materials and products – TFRC's expertise and methods evolve a vision with VF Corporation

Brief:

'This has been a dream project to work on over the past year – it has given us an opportunity to really show how our research can be applied in a range of commercial contexts in ways that are both inspiring and informative. VF commissioned TFRC to help them understand and demonstrate how to use sustainability as a driver for innovation.

'VF had the visionary idea of developing and hosting an innovation showcase, bringing to life consumer-based trends and key technologies that could influence the development of next-generation apparel. A key aim of this event was to create an interactive environment which allowed VF staff to see and experience new and emerging concepts that would help them to identify innovation opportunities, build new networks, and come away feeling inspired and more knowledgeable.

'TFRC contributed to VF's innovation showcase in a number of ways, including creative direction of the overall event and curation of a section within the show dedicated to sustainable design – this role involved us innovating new product concepts.

'We also helped VF tap into fresh thinking from next generation designers by delivering a student design competition that ran across the University Of The Arts London. The winning results were paraded at a live fashion show. TFRC also led practical workshops that put our sustainable methods into action. Overall, we assembled a formidable team of design-led researchers, designers, students and alumni, covering all aspects of our philosophy – sustainable design, scientific collaboration, technical and social innovation and well-being.'

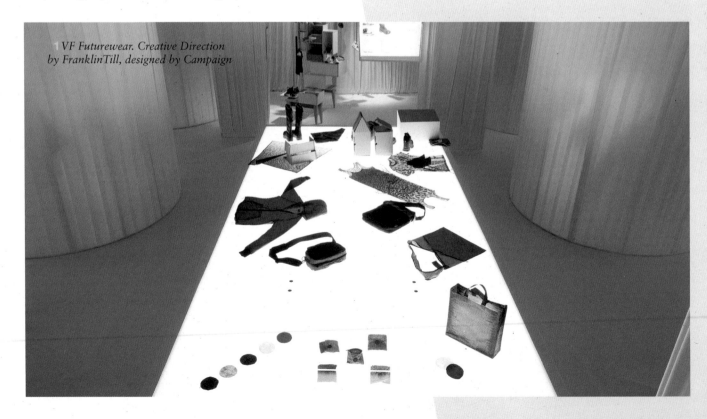

1 *VF Futurewear. Creative Direction by FranklinTill, designed by Campaign*

Process:

The exhibition curation process involved researching existing prototypes to exhibit, as well as conceiving and producing new prototypes in order to realise the vision and potential of the event. The curators and co-curators also mentored many of the designers through the production phase.

TFRC's research was used in myriad ways. The TED group used TED's TEN methods, tools and resources in workshops and design brainstorms to create a tailored and holistic approach to sustainable design for VF. Other researchers were commissioned to apply their recent breakthroughs to specific products and brands.

Caroline Till, co-founder of FranklinTill and TFRC associate researcher, creatively directed the project. FranklinTill worked closely with Campaign and VF on the design, build and creation of the overall exhibition experience. The creation of the hand-held audio tour guide brought each exhibit to life through film and audio.

TFRC commissions:

1

Scent Rucksack

Jenny Tillotson designed 'Lift My Mind', a sports endurance running collection. It offers the selective electronic delivery of multiple scents from a disposable solid-scent cartridge system designed by Ceroma Limited (University Of Cambridge). The project uses scents with recognised properties, such as peppermint, which increases speed, mental performance and cognitive functioning, and lavender for relaxation.

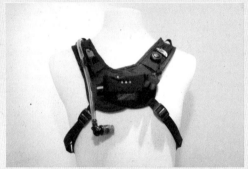

2

Beauty And Utility

Kay Politowicz worked with Sandy MacLennan from East Central Studios to produce a selection of short-life workwear and fashion garments using non-woven materials. The result was 'Beauty And Utility' which adapted unconventional materials, including wet wipes, to construct Once, a single-use fashion T-shirt, while Tuta, a one-piece worksuit, was made from a thermo-bonded non-woven fabric.

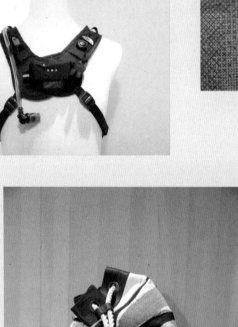

3

Bio Bags

Suzanne Lee created a product range made from a new material that was 'grown' from her mixture of green tea, sugar and various micro-organisms. Under the influence of heat, the fermentation process enables the bacterium to form a cellulose layer, which she dried into workable material to create a collection of purses and bags.

Design For Change

Clara Vuletitch developed a social innovation model to create a new product collection using denim waste. She developed the model in consultation with field experts – Tom Rowley (The Pipeline Project) and Burak Cakmak – and produced three concept bags using factory waste, off-cuts and end-of-roll denim, to encourage staff and consumer participation in the manufacturing phase.

4

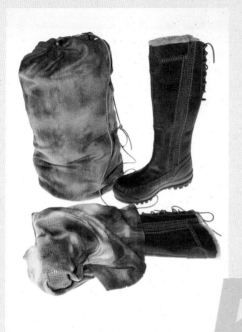

5

Box-Plus and Box-Less

Rebecca Earley and TED research assistant Miriam Ribul developed a range of concepts for consumers and retailers to gain added value from the transportation, storage and take-home experience of footwear. They worked on the brief of transformable packaging with professional designers and students from the University Of The Arts London MA Textiles, Industrial Design and Graphic Design courses to produce prototypes for reducing the amount of waste generated by packaging.

6

Make It Mine

Melanie Bowles created a design system that helped consumers to create their own printed checked fabric and even their own shirt, using little more than marker pens and their mobile phone.

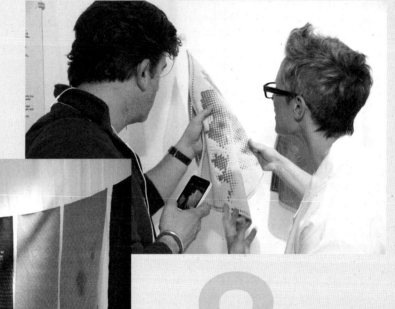

8

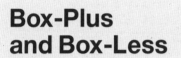

7

Long-Life Denim

Philippa Brock created the 'Cherish' collection – a series of long-life woven denim samples that used a two- or three-layered structure of varying fibres. Exhibition visitors were able to use abrasive tools to wear away the multi-layered denim fabrics, revealing hidden patterns underneath.

Laser Line

Kate Goldsworthy was commissioned to make a bespoke jacket using industrial laser technology to creatively 'weld' end-of-life polyester fabrics together, using programmed images. David Telfer made the 'zero waste' jacket by adapting one of VF's existing patterns.

Debrief:

'The Textile Futures Research Centre really impressed us with their vision, the professionalism of their approach and the range and quality of their expertise and delivery. After a global review of current textiles research we were lucky to be able to work with the UAL's design researchers for the VF innovation showcase.

'From the way they steered the concepts, found innovative content and enthusiastic exhibitors, to contextualising the work for presentation to our brands – TFRC are excellent researchers in their field. They have a unique approach to using technology breakthroughs fused with sustainable design thinking, which many of our brands found really relevant and inspiring.'

Stephen Dull, Senior Vice President
Marty Lawrence, General Manager
Of Innovation VF Corporation

VF Futurewear, Creative Direction
by FranklinTill, designed by Campaign

I want my futurewear to be ___
I want my futurewear to be ___
I want my futurewear to be ___
I want my futurewear to be ___
I want my futurewear to be ___
I want my futurewear to be ___
I want my futurewear to be ___
I want my futurewear to be ___
I want my futurewear to be ___
I want my futurewear to be ___
I want my futurewear to be ___
I want my futurewear to be ___
I want my futurewear to be ___
I want my futurewear to be ___
I want my futurewear to be ___

Sensory Well-Being

Still from Ashtüblif film by Hélène Combal-Weiss

Sensory Well-Being

Despite major advances in medicine and healthcare, modern lifestyles have resulted in obese populations, spiraling rates of heart disease and cancer, rising rates of depression and soaring healthcare costs in countries around the world. Marie O'Mahony explores multi-sensory design approaches to the enhancement of emotional and physical well-being as people increasingly take health and wellness into their own hands

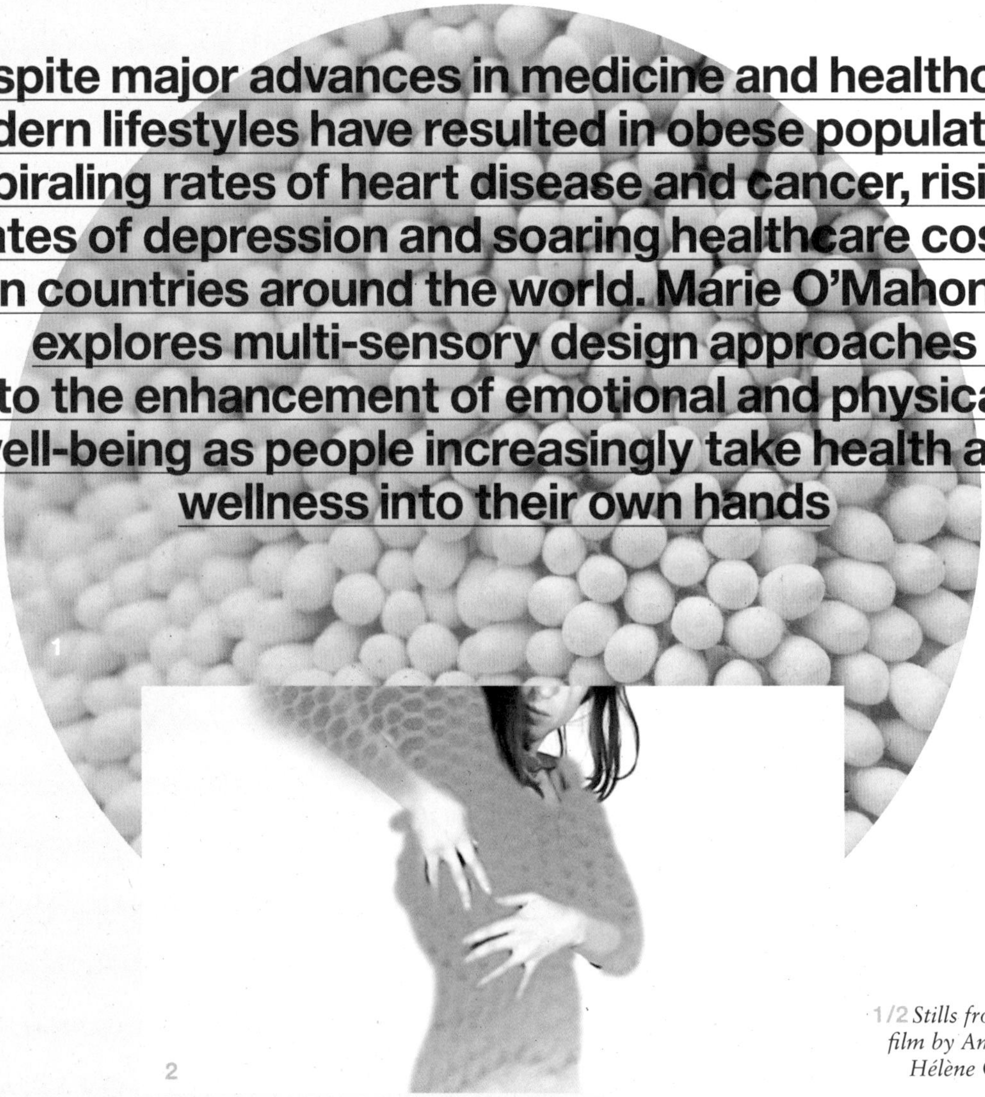

1

2

1/2 Stills from 'Nomadology' film by Amy Radcliffe and Hélène Combal-Weiss

One of the most significant changes in the arena of healthcare over the past decade is the move towards preventative and home care. Wellness is a keystone in this development, which is driven in large part by changing demographics. People are living longer and they want to live more independent lives. The promotion and maintenance of health has been moving outside traditional hospitals and care centres, bringing people back to their homes where they can recover and rebuild their health in familiar surroundings. Remote monitoring, protection from infection and promotion of emotional and physical well-being are an increasing part of this – and textiles are at the forefront of material selection.

Textiles by their nature are extremely adaptable, as fibres, yarns and fabric structures can be highly engineered to allow the material to act as a conduit for other technologies such as scent. As an interface, they have positive user associations in healthcare and wellness, so that the incorporation of additional sensory qualities is an extension of an already positive image. New technologies such as nanotechnology and micro-encapsulation mean that climate control, anti-bacterial and perfumed fabrics can withstand repeated washing and wearing without loss or degeneration. What is emerging is an exciting and vibrant field of textile development that offers the consumer performance and protection alongside, and even incorporating, multisensory textiles.

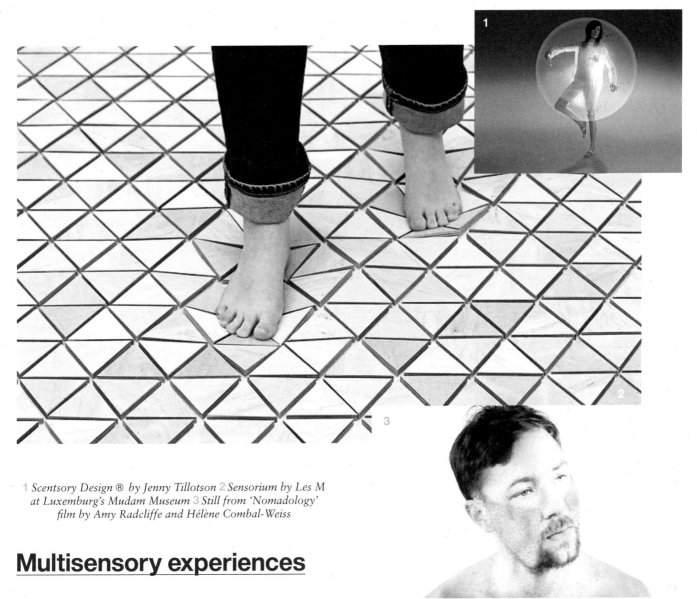

1 *Scentsory Design ® by Jenny Tillotson* 2 *Sensorium by Les M at Luxemburg's Mudam Museum* 3 *Still from 'Nomadology' film by Amy Radcliffe and Hélène Combal-Weiss*

Multisensory experiences

Multisensory experiences are already recognised by forward-thinking designers as a way to encourage new ways of relating to the senses. San Francisco's Exploratorium Museum is home to the Tactile Dome interactive experience; visitors feel their way through the exhibit where light is excluded and 'touch becomes your only guide'.

The Sensorium show at the Mudam museum in Luxembourg similarly invited visitors to explore their sense of touch, along with smell and taste. The exhibit was put together by design duo Céline Merhand and Anaïs Morel, together known as Les M, working with other guest collaborators. Rather than forbidding visitors to touch the exhibit, Merhand and Morel carefully chose the most tactile surfaces and textures they could, and also offered a series of events and workshops, each devoted to one of the five senses. Sensorium presented 'sensual experiences and sensorial surprises that enrich the sixth sense of artistic pleasure.'

Studio Toogood, based in London, also emphasised the multisensory experience in La Cura, a 'hospital for the senses' created for MOST 2012 in Milan. La Cura featured a therapeutic sound and light installation created in collaboration with cross-disciplinary installation artists Kite & Laslett, a special scent devised by perfumers 12.29 and a 're-energising elixir' made by food designers Arabeschi di Latte. Visitors were seated on Studio Toogood's Spade chairs, which were wrapped in bandages, while they moulded a piece of white clay to contribute to a collaborative sculpture that grew as the week-long installation progressed.

Scent for well-being

The senses are not always easy to isolate; they all work together and smell plays a key role. Our sense of smell informs other senses through a direct connection to the limbic system, the portion of the brain that controls the emotions. The human experience of taste, pain and temperature are all informed by smell. Human olfactory cells are capable of detecting thousands of different smells. They affect our health and well-being both directly and through associations personal to each individual's life experience and memories. The relationship between health and odours has been known for some time. As early as the fourth century BC, Hippocrates recognised their importance in diagnosing ailments.

Medical researchers today have found that smell can be used as a formal diagnostic test for certain illnesses, such as schizophrenia and depression, where patients commonly exhibit olfactory deficit or dysfunction. Odours warn of danger, calm the nerves and can help to achieve balance in the nervous system. Advances in diagnostic research are formalising and adding to this knowledge of the power of perfume. Alongside this, the emergence of a range of new technologies is helping facilitate the incorporation of scent into clothing, products, buildings and even the cars that we drive. Textiles are proving key to many of these applications.

Sfumato garment by Yesenia Thibault-Picazo

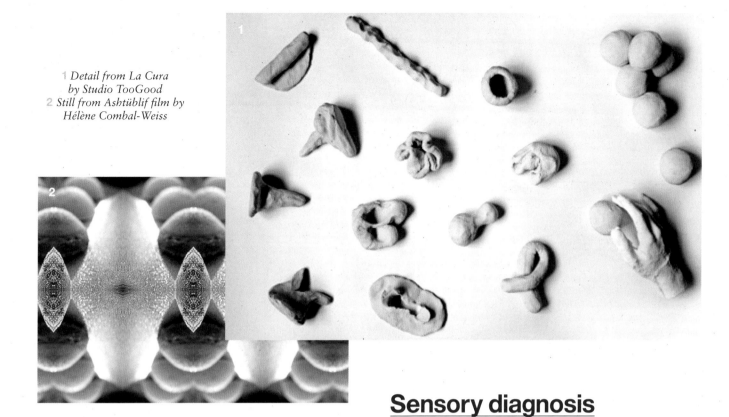

1 *Detail from La Cura*
  by Studio TooGood
2 *Still from Ashtüblif film by*
  Hélène Combal-Weiss

Scentsory Design ®

Dr Jenny Tillotson is a Senior Research Fellow in the Textile Futures Research Centre at Central Saint Martins College as well as a visiting scholar at the Department Of Chemical Engineering And Biotechnology (previously the Institute Of Biotechnology) at the University Of Cambridge. Her particular area of expertise is the application of novel ways to create interactive textile structures that can release a range of personalised scents on demand; although Tillotson suggests that the term 'multi-sensory textiles' can be 'a bit misleading as it can it can mean so many things in the sensory field if you delve into sensory processing disorders and synaesthesia, etc.'

Such delving has focused Tillotson's research on olfaction and emotion, alongside the more obvious sensory effects that she identifies in textiles – visual, textural and auditory. Her interest came about through giving emotional support to people with mental health issues and those living with HIV/Aids. This experience developed into a vision of creating interactive textiles capable of offering support through healing, wellness-enhancing scents. She describes her research as 'fusing the old with the new: the ancient art of perfumery with emerging technologies.' She combines academia (Central Saint Martins) with industry (in association with Philips) in what could be termed a creative convergence of different disciplines and approaches.

The role that Tillotson sees for multi-sensory textiles is for mood enhancement and pain relief. She envisages a future where textiles can capture and process 'smell memories', believing that this has potential for the treatment of dementia and also for 'reminiscence therapy'. Her current focus is on new delivery and sensing systems. Tillotson's recently completed Knowledge Transfer Fellowship with Philips, which was funded by the Arts & Humanities Research Council, looked at colour and scent in 'emotional' jewellery and products; she suggests that future applications for this work might include reducing stress and enhancing sleep with multi-sensory textiles.

Sensory diagnosis

Dr Jenny Tillotson believes that we are at the point of needing some help with our sensory perception. In prehistoric times, she says, humans relied heavily on modes of sensory perception that are now underused: cognition of barely perceptible changes of light, colour, smell and touch were essential to keep our ancestors alive. Their sensory appreciation taught them how to sniff out disease, sense danger, know what foods to avoid, know when to sow and reap, even when to reproduce. 'Animals still rely on personally discriminating those changes,' says Tillotson. 'We humans have not lost those faculties but due to excessive information overload, or "data smog", we have grown to rely on data presented to us in other ways.'

Sophisticated sensor technology and nanotechnologies are possible ways to enhance – and even replace – some of our sensory perception in the future. A research team at the University of Warwick is developing a combined electronic nose and tongue, using ChemFET sensors for the 'nose' and shear horizontal surface acoustic wave (SH-SAW) sensors for the 'tongue'. Combining the two types of sensor is intended is to combine the effects of nasal and oral stimulation to assess flavour experienced by smell and taste in combination. Nanotechnology is being used by Nano Engineered Applications Inc. to develop a prototype e-nose. This development, which uses functionalized carbon nanotubes about 100,000 times finer than human hair, has potential applications in the detection of airborne toxins and gas leaks.

Other designers are also turning to technology to produce applications that will enhance human sensory perception. The Apothecary, featured on the Design Probes page of the Philips far-future research dialogue website, lets users analyse the state of their health using four diagnostic tools that test breath, tongue, skin and eyes; breath and saliva testing give an indication of the state of intestinal flora, while optical scans and skin surface tests provide other metrics for 'slow diagnosis'. Susana Soares' Bee's project uses bees to detect health issues by using their acute olfactory systems to smell human breath blown through a specially designed vessel. According to Soares, bees can be trained using Pavlov's reflex to respond to a wide range of natural and man-made chemicals and odours, including the biomarkers associated with certain diseases.

Blending the senses

As we have seen, the senses are closely interlinked, and artists and designers are drawing on that synergy in a variety of ways. Neil Harbisson, an artist who has been colour-blind since birth, has been working with computer scientists since 2003 on a project designed to enable him to 'hear' colour (TED Global 2012). Harbisson can now experience different colours by equating them with a particular sound. The fact that he can now dream in colour and 'listen' to a Picasso painting in a museum is a measure of the success of the project. He has been allowed to appear in his passport photograph wearing the device that enables this, as he argues this is part of him. This is an important move in the acceptance and de-stigmatisation of enabling technologies.

1 *Sensorium by Les M at Luxemburg's Mudam Museum* 2 *The Transformative Chronotype by Julie Yonehara*

Harnessing the healing power of colour and light, The Transformative Chronotype by Julie Yonehara, an MA Textile Futures graduate from CSM, explores the manipulation of the human circadian rhythm. It is designed as a vanity set; eye masks engineer the level of sedative red light that reaches the eyes, helping the user relax, while a make-up compact emits light with interchangeable filters to adjust the level of energising blue light received.

ChromoTM, by Hideaki Matsui and Momo Miyazaki, students at the Copenhagen Institute of Interaction Design, also draws on the idea of 'hearing' colours, using software to translate colours into audible musical notes to create a 'colour clock' to combat jet lag, seasonal affective disorder and other disorders related to light levels and time. Matsui and Miyazaki were inspired by research that suggests colours and light play a central role in balancing mood by regulating body clocks, and ChromoTM is intended to help release the right hormone at the right time.

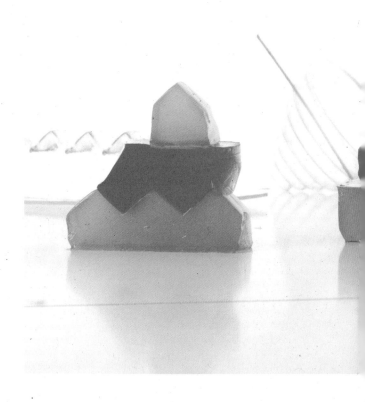

Noisy Jelly by Marianne Cauvard and Raphaël Pluvinage, students at ENSCI Les Ateliers, plays with the concept of audible colour; users make colourful jellies which release musical sounds based on their shape, size, salt concentration and how forcefully they are touched.

Digital well-being

Digital sensorial devices and interactive systems can also be used to enhance day-to-day well-being. Philips' goLite Blu light also uses the energy-enhancing properties of blue light, producing a particular kind of pure blue light that occurs naturally on very sunny, clear days. Special receptors in the eyes absorb this blue light, which lends energy and helps alleviate the 'winter blues' and tiredness from jet lag. The Lapka appcessory for iPhones, described as a 'personal environment monitor', measures atmospheric humidity and temperature, radiation levels, electromagnetic frequency and even features a probe that can test whether food is genuinely organic – the steel probe can check the concentration of nitrates, commonly used in manufactured fertilisers.

The Channel Of Mindfulness meditation wheel, also created for use with the iPhone, plays sounds to assist in meditation when the user swings it rhythmically. Yufan Wang's design is loosely based on that of the Tibetan prayer wheel. 'Channel Of Mindfulness creates a new way to help inexperienced practitioners to discover and integrate mindfulness in their everyday life,' says Wang. 'The idea is to help people live in the moment through listening and concentrating on meditative sounds.' Perhaps the Channel Of Mindfulness would make a good partner for Flowtime, an interactive electronic top with accompanying software that helps yoga practitioners synchronise breath and movement. Flowtime was developed by Ralf Zoontjens in a study of wearable electronics at the department of industrial design, Eindhoven University Of Technology. 'Technology becomes a peripheral signal that recedes into the background of awareness, and helps people become one with their body and mind,' says Zoontjens.

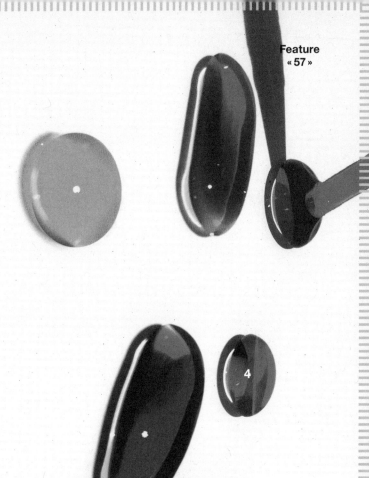

3 *Noisy Jelly by Marianne Cauvard*
and Raphaël Pluvinage
4 *Audible Colour by Hideaki Matsui*
and Momo Miyazaki, students
at the Copenhagen Institute
of Interaction Design

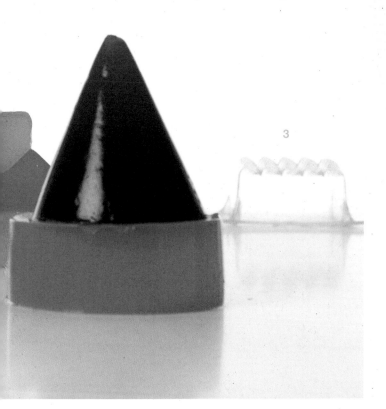

3

Conclusion

There are many ways in which the senses can be employed in multisensory innovations for health and well-being. The inherent visual, aural and tactile qualities of materials are being coupled with the new possibilities offered by scent and its enabling technologies. Developments in textiles are being combined with new research in medicine, sportswear, space and other disciplines into the role of clothing and environment on health and well-being. This is leading to new ways that the disciplines themselves can work together. Many of the examples discussed here involve researchers and practitioners from several disciplines, including academia, science, medicine and industry. What is becoming increasingly rare are single disciplines that can house all of the skills and knowledge necessary to develop these materials.

Innovation is emerging from small start-ups as well as large corporations, universities and cross-discipline teams. The demand for multi-sensory textiles for health and well-being is here, and will remain well into the future. There is only one question. Who is ready to rise to the challenge?

The Future Of Sustainable Mobility

Biologically engineered material, transformable structures, nomadic lifestyles, community systems and the experiential journey were among the themes explored by first-year MA Textile Futures students during a collaborative project with Nissan Design Europe

MA Textile Futures is a two-year master's programme based at Central Saint Martins College Of Arts And Design. Textile Futures students, who essentially practise research-driven design, are encouraged to rethink the future of our material world, looking beyond existing scientific and technological developments to meet future needs, desires and challenges.

Nissan Design Europe approached the Textile Futures course staff, asking them to consider far-future concepts for sustainable mobility that could form part of an internal exhibition to inform and inspire Nissan staff globally. Twenty-one first-year students were involved in the initial stages of the project and four project concepts were selected to be taken forward for exhibition.

Students are encouraged to rethink the future of our material world

The Textile Futures group was invited to transport its studio to Nissan for the day and the students spent the morning exploring the company's various departments, learning more about the automotive industry and design process. This led into a brainstorm session to generate ideas for the future of sustainable mobility.

Following a dynamic session rich in ideas, four students were selected to develop concepts around some of the key themes that emerged from the session, building sketchbooks, visualisations and prototypes which were to be exhibited in the Nissan studios later in the year.

Grow Your Own

Grow Your Own Car? – part of Amy Congdon's work for Nissan Design Europe

Nissan design studios are laboratories where new materials and shapes are developed and genetically tested. The best structural features of nature are used to produce the strongest new composites. For example, bacteria are used to cover template forms with abalone skeletons and genetically altered lichen grows over the frame to convert harmful gases into fuel for the cars. This new system drastically reduces the resources used in the chain of manufacture and, as such, is as close to a zero-waste production model as possible

Rethinking mobility

Amy Congdon proposed a future scenario in which biology could become one of the new vectors of engineering. In this imagined future vehicles could be constructed to order, grown in vats or from seeds, and developed by designers, engineers and scientists working in close collaboration.

Miriam Ribul explored future community tribes and transformable structures to encourage car-sharing schemes, while Natsai Chieza explored the revived importance of the driving experience in a future in which teleportation has become the major means of mobility.

Equally blue-sky in approach, Ann-Kristin Abel suggested that collation, curation and storage of information will be key to enabling mobility in a world that has become increasingly nomadic. She communicated her vision of the Plasmorph, 'a living diary that provides customised and instant information to its user by ingesting it directly into the nervous system.'

The Plasmorph by Ann-Kristin Abel for Nissan Design Europe

The Plasmorph device is a semi-being, a biological prosthesis that extends the human body to the virtual realm. The hybrid organism senses your interests and builds up your experience and your memories. It is a living diary and provides customised and instant information to its user by ingesting it directly into the nervous system. The growth happens by 'feeding' your Plasmorph with human encounters, memories and emotions

Craft

bricolage•

Engagement

Craft Engagement

As craft weaves its way into popular culture, Grant Gibson and M Astella Saw examine how designers and makers are collaborating to create our communal future

Community quilting at a Bricolage workshop

Craft is coming out of the garden shed, out of the spare room – out of the closet. For a new generation of amateur seamstresses, knitters, crocheters, builders, hackers and all-round DIY enthusiasts, hands-on craft, rather than being a solitary hobby, is a means of forming new communities. Weaned on the social internet – where sewing patterns and building plans are easily shared, where a question about purling technique can be rapidly answered on an online forum – these 20- and 30-somethings are driven by a desire to learn and engage socially with craft. By redefining craft as a communal activity, today's craft practitioners are weaving together the common threads of future crafting.

Slowing down

The desire to engage with craft is in part a modern offshoot of the Slow movement, a grassroots revolution of sorts that gained popularity in the late 20th century as consumers began to approach food, travel and design in a slower, more thoughtful, often more communal manner. 'Making is a process of thinking,' says Linda Florence, a designer and senior lecturer of BA Textiles at Central Saint Martins. 'In a culture where we often look for instant gratification, making is about taking time to learn a skill and develop it. Quite often [craft] can be about process and not the final outcome.'

Crafting real connections

Furthermore, craft – specifically craft practised communally – speaks to people's desire for physical connections and community in an increasingly virtual world, says Textile Futures Research Centre (TFRC) associate member Clara Vuletich, who is a founder of Bricolage, a collective of textile designers formed in 2009. The collective organises community workshops to teach what Vuletich describes as 'resilient skills for a changing world' – practical skills, that is, such as darning, mending, knitting, crochet, patchworking and quilting. Workshop attendees are 'professional people who need something else in their private lives', Vuletich says. Many of them come from design backgrounds and spend much of their time alone, staring at computer screens – a feeling with which Vuletich has some empathy. Overwhelmed by 'an overload of digital information', people find that making can be a coping mechanism, she says.

Popular crafts

As people search for ways to disconnect, communal crafting speaks to the zeitgeist. At the Drink, Shop & Do café in London and at De Nieuwe Anita, a bar and music venue in Amsterdam, bright young things are forming contemporary versions of 19th-century quilting bees and sewing circles. In Los Angeles, Melbourne and Seoul, guerrilla knitters, or yarn bombers, collaborate with local communities to create public art installations, covering anything from lampposts to abandoned bicycles in colourful bits of unfinished knitting or crocheted squares. Elsewhere, members of the Bleeding Thumb Whittling Club in east London gather once a month to carve diverse and curious objects, while the Hyperbolic Crochet Coral Reef project, which began in the living room of Margaret and Christine Wertheim in Queensland, Australia, in 2005, now brings together communities of makers and scientists across the globe.

Even consumer brands not traditionally associated with craft have come to support the creative social movement in its various iterations. Clothing brand Diesel's Bling For Good upcycling project sees jewellery designers hosting workshops in Berlin, Düsseldorf and Hamburg to teach people how to create accessories from unwanted materials such as old T-shirts, rivets and zippers. Similarly, jeans brand Levi's organised a series of workshops for collaboration and creative production, including one on photography in New York, one on filmmaking in Los Angeles, and two on printmaking in London and Berlin.

1 Wandering Methods by Linda Florence photography by Lian Bell 2 Threads and Yarns Workshop at the V&A organised by Jo Morrison & Anne Marr

Sharing challenges, sharing skills

One of the most rewarding aspects of collaborative crafting – one reason why communal crafting appeals – is the exchange of knowledge between participants, practitioners say. 'Each group of people I have worked with has brought a wealth of knowledge, experience and skills to the project, and learned and developed their own skills as the project has taken place,' says CSM's Linda Florence, whose recent collaborations have helped nurture a sense of community through participation in a shared activity. 'There have been challenges working on outcomes within a group, and debate and reflection over making and ownership on projects.'

In May 2012, with artist Maeve Clancy and a group of local residents, Florence organised the Wandering Methods project, developed by Bealtaine Festival and crafts development organisation Craftspace in partnership with the Irish Office of Public Works, to interpret the history, stories and architecture of Rathfarnham Castle outside Dublin. Using photography, drawing, monoprinting and screenprinting, the group produced individual papercuts and two wallpaper designs that combined everyone's drawings. An earlier project, Time in Print, developed with Craftspace and UK conservation charity the National Trust, similarly saw Florence work with Wolverhampton residents to explore the stories behind local historic home Wightwick Manor. Alongside local residents of Afro-Caribbean heritage, Florence helped develop a number of contemporary wallpapers and prints inspired by the property's Arts and Crafts interior and collections. 'I've never seen a group get quite so enthusiastic,' Florence says, of the Wandering Methods participants and their response to communal crafting. 'They wanted to take stuff home to do and come back the next day.'

The fabrics of our lives

In her research into collaborative textile craft practice, TFRC research student Susan Noble, a principal lecturer at the School Of Art, Design And Media at the University Of Portsmouth, has found that many domestic crafts readily lend themselves to communal activity. 'Patchwork has traditionally been community based, but it's also amazing how quickly knitting circles spring up, even though knitting is an individual activity,' Noble says. 'There's something about the process that seems to engender community – maybe because it's more purposeful than just sitting around drinking tea and socialising.'

Over the past six years, Noble's project, The Craft Circle, brought together a group of elderly local women and university students, who gathered to practise traditional crafting skills such as knitting. The weekly meetings quickly progressed from knowledge-sharing to the forming of real bonds, with students wanting to be paired with the same partner they had worked with the previous week. 'Everyone got very comfortable with each other,' Noble says. 'They'd look out for each other.'

A similar project, Threads And Yarns, led by Central Saint Martins digital projects director Jo Morrison and BA Textiles course leader Anne Marr, in partnership with the V&A Museum and the Wellcome Trust, also saw communal crafting – and the chit-chat that comes with it – at work. In this intergenerational textile project, senior citizens from north London and further afield worked with first-year students from Central Saint Martins BA Textile Design course in a series of craft workshops, during which they also discussed their personal experiences of health and well-being. Art and craft therapy is an established practice in the mental health profession to help improve patients' well-being; in Threads and Yarns, such art and craft practice also proved itself useful in informing how future textile design research can provide a response to social and community issues.

Creative collaboration

As communal crafting continues to gain adherents, new ways of working within the increasingly collaborative creative industries will present themselves. 'It will be really interesting to see how we collaborate,' Noble says. 'Within an academic situation, a commercial one or an artistic one, people normally have distinctive roles. I want to look at how we work when that role isn't so clear. The elderly women I'm working with are much more instinctive, much more intuitive. For them, craft has more to do with motivation – the effects that craft making has. For a designer to be so un-outcome driven is unusual. To look at craft as a state of mind is fascinating.'

1 *Wandering Methods by Linda Florence, photography by Lian Bell* 2 *Taking Time Craft and the Slow Revolution at The National Trust and Birmingham Museum and Art Gallery, Birmingham by Linda Florence*

New old generations

Going beyond matters of best practice, communal crafting has a real potential to evolve as a force for social good. 'Social engagement projects including cross-generational learning and collaborative making will become very important for well-being as our society ages,' Linda Florence says. 'With more of us expected to reach our hundredth birthday, it has never been more important to address the issues faced by elders within our community, including isolation and mental health issues. We can enrich learning experiences by engaging with people who have a lifetime of experience to pass on to others through collaborative projects.'

Craft knowledge – the traditional skills and know-how that come woven into the phrase – has always quietly passed from one generation to another, stitch by stitch, etch by etch, with people working side by side. Today's generation of socially minded designers and makers continues that tradition. Fascinated by the collaborative process, imbued with a sense of social engagement and keen to make connections within their communities, craft practitioners are once again gathering around

MISTRA Future Fashion 2011-15

Towards Systemic Change For Swedish Fashion

How can sustainable design processes be created and embedded within companies and gain the participation of consumers? Within the MISTRA Future Fashion project, the Textiles Environment Design group aims to develop design thinking by involving a wider range of stakeholders across the fashion industry, including design, retail, CSR and marketing. The project will encourage involvement in the design process and build a more meaningful interface between retailer and consumer

Burak Cakmak, Anna Palme and Gustav Sandin at TED's Summer Workshop 2012, photography by José Farinha

Becky Earley, Director TFRC:

'MISTRA Future Fashion (MFF) has been one of Textiles Environment Design's major projects since 2011 and it's been such a pleasure to work within a partnership of designers, scientists, and business people, each lending their skills and analysis to the consortium. TED is leading Project 3 where our objective is to improve product and service development processes – we aim for significantly better environmental performance achieved through design.

'The TED team are delighted to be given an opportunity to use our sustainable design strategies as a basis for developing a really exciting programme aimed at design, CSR and marketing professionals within the fashion and textile industry. It includes a training scheme for design staff at H&M; a new online platform where we'll create and disseminate research findings and launch design opportunities. We have already given a multitude of international presentations – in Boston, Gothenburg, Copenhagen, Milan, and London. The project also gives us a PhD scholarship and a Guest Professorship at Konstfack in Stockholm.

'We're currently developing an online exhibition showcasing new prototypes and concepts, which will be accompanied by real-time interactive workshops inviting public participation and feedback. Also in the pipeline is an industry report and a final digital outcome where we'll summarise our findings to create a self-sustaining legacy for the design world.'

1 Educating the next generation

Through art and design education, individuality, imagination and innovation are encouraged and developed within the student experience. Intelligent investigation of ideas stimulates thoughtful and playful solutions to environmental, economic and social questions that are facing society in the 21st century. TED's model of practice-led research transforms theories into actions in a 'thinking through making' approach. Design and reflection are connected, to involve students, practitioners, and researchers in collaborative practice. TED's TEN provides a framework for philosophical development and practical action, which introduces students to a way of finding an individual approach to innovation within a professional real-world context.

2 Training design professionals

TED's TEN offers an accessible way for designers to scope the sustainability landscape, allowing them to quickly grasp information to enable them to arrive at ideas for new products and services. Since 2006 we have been developing workshop techniques that take the designers on a journey through a range of approaches, resulting in a 'layering' of their ideas for improvement together. This experience often gives the participants a new way of viewing the design process, and for the MISTRA project we are working with a range of Swedish designers on a bespoke experience to help them meet the demands that systemic change will require.

3 Model for social textiles

Taking several of the TED's TEN strategies as a starting point, this project explores ways that fashion and textile designers can bring about positive societal change. Currently the contributions that designers in the fashion industry make towards creating social change are limited to choosing a supplier who brings fair wages to workers, or supporting small, craft-based producer communities. Designers in other disciplines are proactively using their design skills for community engagement projects or working in the social innovation sector; this project will examine how fashion and textile designers could do the same. It will also explore the new skills or tools that a fashion/textile designer might need to become a facilitator/activist.

4 Connecting communities online

Textiletoolbox.com is an open innovation platform that connects contributions from leading academics, researchers and designers to build a resource for key stakeholders from the Swedish fashion industry. The site alsos engage with consumers and allow feedback from external contributors. This open innovation platform embeds the TED's TEN strategies in the Swedish fashion landscape through inspirational examples and thought-provoking texts. In the future it will include interviews with fashion and textiles professionals about the key challenges they face when aiming to embed sustainability in their companies. The legacy of this open innovation platform will be a resource for designers and consumers on how to work practically towards systemic change.

"At the Sustainable Fashion Academy in Stockholm we discovered that working with Becky and her team using TED's ideas offered a really informative, inspiring and accessible way for our designers to grasp the broad landscape of sustainable design. In a short space of time we found creative ways to make product and service innovations. Through the MISTRA project we are now looking at research that will enable us to tailor TED's TEN to approach a very specific set of questions" Johan Ward, H&M

Rebecca Earley at H&M,
photography by H&M

Textile Toolbox

Textile Toolbox is the home of TED's ongoing project with MISTRA Future Fashion in Sweden, a consortium which aims to create systemic change within the industry. The website is a platform where participants and audience can engage with new ideas. It is being used to help build the discourse around TED's TEN, a set of sustainable design strategies which drive innovative action, applying them to aspects of the Swedish fashion industry. The blog posts generated will eventually form the basis of a report that TED will publish in 2013.

Textiletoolbox.com will rely on the contribution of experts from different disciplines, chosen by TED and including Jonathan Chapman, Otto von Busch, and Sandy MacLennan. It will study how lower impacts within the fashion and textiles industry can be achieved by challenging the aesthetic, lifecycle and production issues around a variety of products. Each section, led by one or more of our experts, will contribute key case studies and interviews with leading industry stakeholders. The content will focus on inspirational projects – but also on the challenges the industry faces.

The outcomes will be published in our final report in 2015. Follow our progress and send feedback through Twitter. News and updates are available by signing up to the mailing list at textiletoolbox.com

Dream
Factory

Paper Fashion by Kay Politowicz and Sandy MacLennan, photography by Aaron Tilley

With turbulent times possibly ahead, designers and makers are rethinking the systems that feed and clothe us – the very systems on which our everyday lives are based. Clara Vuletich checks out the alternatives

SpiderFarm by Thomas Maincent

Each week, it seems, a new report is released that shows how systems supporting life on this planet – soils, oceans, forests – are under threat. Further, in the global recession, the world's poorest are getting poorer: the World Bank has estimated that, in developing countries, the number of people living on less than US$10 a day is equivalent to 80 percent of the world's population. Overwhelmed by such facts and figures, some people would be inclined to turn their heads and continue with business as usual.

Not so for a new breed of designers and companies who are reimagining what design for the environment and for people means. Working collaboratively with scientists, the not-for profit sector and new technology, these designers and makers are changing the "brown paper" image of sustainable design, imaginatively transforming the field to one that sees sustainability as an opportunity for radical innovation and creativity. Welcome to the Dream Factory.

Systems thinking

In an increasingly transparent world, we now have easy access to details of product lifecycles, such as factory locations and material toxicity. Rather than getting lost in the big picture, designers and companies are using this information to empower themselves, pairing this learning with data on global poverty to create products and systems that work in harmony with nature, and to offer alternatives to mass production.

In 'The Machine: Designing A New Industrial Revolution', an exhibition in Genk, Belgium, in summer 2012, a group of designers created a series of machines to help shape the future of production and consumption. One 'factory' reconstructed the environmental conditions of a spider's habitat to spin spider silk, while another demonstrated a versatile and low-tech way to produce organically shaped plastic vases. In effect, the designers took on a similar role to the one engineers had in the first industrial revolution: they became systems designers who built their own machines and showed us how they work.

Self-sustaining systems

The notion of designing new systems is already informing projects dealing with urban food production. While the current industrial food system is designed to feed billions of people, the resilience of the system – with its reliance on fossil fuels, pesticides and air freight – is questionable. Plus, with more of the world's population moving into cities, designers and entrepreneurs are exploring localised, self-sustaining ways of growing food and building resilient communities.

Aquaponics, the cultivation of fish and plants together in a constructed, recirculating ecosystem, has captured the imagination of many urban farm advocates. In aquaponics gardening, natural bacteria cycles convert fish waste to plant nutrients. Amsterdam publisher and cultural institution Mediamatic is exploring aquaponics in its headquarters in former ship-building halls just outside the centre of the city. Staff and members of the organisation have designed and constructed an aquaponics system from plastic bins and a simple metal frame. In order to share the knowledge gained from this DIY experiment, they also organise workshops for people wanting to build their own aquaponics system at home.

Meanwhile, a group of agro-entrepreneurs in Berlin are transforming a former malt factory into a sustainable farm, also using aquaponics to raise fish and grow vegetables. Frisch Vom Dach (Fresh From The Roof) will comprise a 7,000-square-metre roof garden, with the fish contained in the old vats once used to dry barley. The enterprise is being set up as a fully financed business, and the entrepreneurs hope to start selling their produce to the local community by 2013.

1 *Spid Aquaponics Workshop by Mediamatics at the Transnatural Festival, Amsterdam*

Alternative energy

Elsewhere, faced with the increasing need for energy efficiency and the demand for alternatives to non-renewable resources such as petroleum, designers and scientists are investigating new ways to produce and harvest energy.

Led by TFRC Deputy Director Carole Collet and Belgium based artist Bartaku the Edible Alchemy project forms part of the Resilients. Initiated by a consortium of 6 cultural organisations in 2010, the Resilients project is supported by the European Culture Programme. The collective objective is to gather, create and support resilient creative practices that can enable humans to thrive in uncertain and turbulent times. The Edible Alchemy project explores models of resilience inspired by two plants, the aronia bush (Aronia melanocarpa) and flax (Linum usitatissimum). The idea is to exploit the potential to transform and adapt one material into as many different design applications as possible. Carole Collet explains 'the project focus involves the production of a table landscape installation celebrating the multifarious possibilities to transform aronia berries and flax into innovative food and design products: from edible photovoltaic aronia tapas, (TpED) that produce micro voltage, to furniture and tableware made form new linen composites.'

Dutch designer Marjan van Aubel is also exploring how everyday objects can generate power. Her Energy Collection features a range of glassware that absorbs energy from daylight. When the glasses are not in use, they are stored in a specially designed cabinet that collects and stores this solar power, and that can later be used, as if it were a huge battery, to charge electrical objects. The concept uses a new technique developed by Swiss scientist Michael Grätzel, who discovered that cells use colour to generate electricity in the same way plants do when they photosynthesise. In each of her glass objects, van Aubel has placed a photovoltaic layer of a dye-synthesised solar cell that will generate an electrical current once it is exposed to sunlight.

*Edible Alchemy: A worklab organised by Bartaku and Carole Collet
as part of Resilients, a European Culture Programme Project.*

2

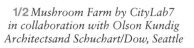

1

*1/2 Mushroom Farm by CityLab7
in collaboration with Olson Kundig
Architectsand Schuchart/Dow, Seattle*

1/2 *Stone Spray Project by Petr Novikov, Anna Kulik, Inder Shergill under the supervision of Marta Malé-Alemany, Jordi Portell and Miquel Lloveras of Institute for Advanced Architecture of Catalonia* 3 *Solar Sinter by Markus Kayser, photography by Amos Field Reid*

New manufacturing

A resilient future is also one where manufacturing techniques are flexible and localised, particularly as access to large-scale manufacturing processes may become difficult or too costly. Designers are exploring the potential of rapid prototyping, or 3D printing, to turn current manufacturing on its head.

Stone Spray is a robotic 3D printer that mixes soil with a liquid binder to create sculptures and architectural shapes, such as temporary canopies or bridges. Unlike most 3D printing technology, the robot can print multidirectionally and is powered by solar energy. The project, by architects Anna Kulik, Inder Shergill and Petr Novikov of the Institute For Advanced Architecture Of Catalonia, was a result of the students' investigations into the on-site digital fabrication of architecture. They chose to work with soil as it is the most commonly found material at building sites; once the Stone Spray structures have been built, the final material is also eco-friendly.

Hanover-born, London-based designer Markus Kayser is also inspired to push the boundaries of 3D print technology for local needs. Tapping into the abundant supplies of sun and sand available in desert regions, his Solar Sinter is a solar-powered machine to make glass objects. In current 3D print technology, a powdery substance is converted into a solid form via sintering – a heating process using laser technology. Kayser's system uses the sun's rays instead of a laser, and sand rather than resins.

Towards a Zero Waste Future: Creating Closed Loop Systems by Dr Kate Goldsworthy

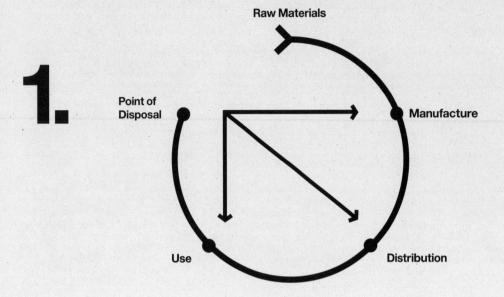

1.

Now
Upcycling by Design

Limited materials with limited life cycles. Although return journeys can be designed at the end-of-life, this approach only postpones the arrival of the discarded material at landfill, where it may never biodegrade, may degrade very slowly or may add harmful materials to the environment as it breaks down.

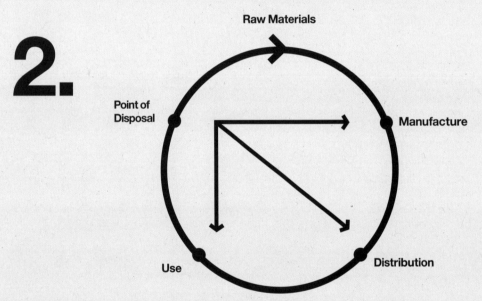

2.

Near
Design for Cradle -2-Cradle

Limited materials with unlimited life cycles. By considering the barriers to recycling as part of the design brief, connected loops can be built into the material's future life from the outset. In a closed-loop, materials would never lose their value and would be designed to be recycled indefinitely.

3.

Future
Design for Material Ecologies

Unlimited materials with unlimited life cycles. A genuinely sustainable future depends on creating interconnected loops, or cycles, for all industrial commodities. These cycles would be part of a scaled up system of material exchange which is open and dynamic, including all material resources in an infinite industrial ecology.

Cyclability

Looking beyond the product to examine the entire system in which a product operates has been a natural progression for Becky Earley, reader in the Textiles Environment Design research group at Camberwell, Chelsea and Wimbledon colleges (TED/CCW). Earley, who is also acting director of the Textile Futures Research Centre (TFRC), has been working at the forefront of design-led textile upcycling for the last 10 years, with her Top 100 polyester shirt project and the Ever & Again: Rethinking Recycled Textiles research project at TED/CCW.

She believes her own practice as a designer reflects the wider shifts towards systems thinking. 'Like other designers exploring textile recycling, I have spent many years proving we can make beautiful garments and objects from waste materials and used garments,' she says. 'These projects demonstrate our creative potential, but they don't demonstrate our economic or environmental potential. They are meaningless until we put them into the bigger systems, which is where my design work is currently heading.'

Earley is currently working with industry partners to explore the potential for the chemical recycling of natural or mixed fibres. Her goal is to eventually create a closed-loop system for natural fibres that could operate at a local, distributed scale.

Systems thinking is also encouraging a growing number of designers to challenge wasteful manufacturing systems that dump valuable materials into landfill, particularly in light of the finite quantities of the earth's resources. These designers see the materials they source and use as part of a continuous cycle that could be reused ad infinitum.

Designing for a closed-loop system is the inspiration for Dr Kate Goldsworthy, senior research fellow at TED/CCW, who is focusing on designing recyclability into polyester. 'I realised early on in my research that most designers who were using waste textiles were merely extending the life of the materials – giving them one more life before they eventually ended up in landfill,' she says. 'But I wanted to know how we could design for recycling, or what I call "forward recycling". This became possible with the introduction of the chemical recycling of polyester back into virgin-quality polyester."

*1 Laser-Finishing of Textiles for a Closed-loop Polyester Economy by Kate Goldsworthy
2/3 Black Hack Workshop by Becky Earley, photography by Mischa Haller*

Although the technology already existed to recycle used polyester, the problem is that most polyester clothes are finished with decorative or functional coatings that render the material unrecyclable. Goldsworthy has solved this problem by using a laser machine to replicate traditional finishing techniques simply by manipulating the surface of the polyester to create 100-percent mono-materiality.

Professor Kay Politowicz, co-founder of TED/CCW, shares this proactive approach to the re-use of materials. Politowicz's most recent project was inspired by the alarming statistic that most of the energy impacts in a garment's life occur when the consumer washes and cares for it. There have been some initiatives by retailers to raise awareness about washing our clothes at lower temperatures, and some advances by manufacturers to make washing machines more efficient. However, Politowicz began to wonder if we could make garments to be worn once, and then recycled. This would save on the energy and water used in washing, and on the vast amounts of textile waste that goes into landfill.

In collaboration with industry partners, Politowicz has developed a range of prototype garments made from a non-woven paper fabric. While the idea may bring visions of the stiff paper dresses from the 1960s, Politowicz is adamant that this proposal is potentially a truly disruptive idea. 'This is not a paper alternative to clothes, but a new approach to meeting a consumer need while also adding some sustainability gains,' she says. 'Most people wouldn't imagine this as a possibility because it's never been offered to them as a viable alternative. There haven't been any developments in paper fabric technology in years, and if designers in the fashion industry haven't got a fabric that feels good and drapes well, they are not going to consider it. But that is not to say it doesn't have great potential.'

Social innovation

Denim Bag Project by Clara Vuletich,
photography by Robert Self

In the last decade, there have been many stories in the fashion and textiles industry of people working in factories under poor conditions, people barely paid a living wage. Many fashion brands and designers have cleaned up their act, but the system still allows for unethical practices. Some designers are taking more radical action by partnering with businesses and non-governmental organisations, and using strategic innovation methods to empower the people who work throughout the supply chain and in local communities.

Mo Tomaney, senior research fellow at Central Saint Martins and a TFRC associate researcher, has visited factories and communities around the world as a consultant on ethical production in the fashion industry. She has witnessed the harsh realities of poverty that most designers never see, and is convinced of the positive role that business can play in these communities. 'I believe in the private sector as a driver for development,' she says. 'I have worked with mills and brands for many years to develop sustainable supply chains and create commercially viable products. My role is to link up the different sectors – NGOs, brands, suppliers and the market.'

In my own PhD research at TED/CCW, part of the MISTRA Future Fashion programme, I consider myself a systems designer, working to intervene in an industry that does not treat the people in the system fairly. I hope to create new models for designers and brands to work toward creating real social change, both at home and abroad. As part of my recent project, Design For Change, I worked with a social business and branding expert to focus on a denim brand manufactured in the USA, developing a model for this brand to take more responsibility in the community in which it is based. We designed a range of fashion accessories made using waste from the production process, partnered with a community group that identified people in need of employment, and trained these people to make the products. All of this was generated from a design hub led by designers from the brand.

Reimagining systems

We are heading into a dynamic period. From past and current methods of manufacturing to the very way in which we live in urban communities, changes are afoot. As environmentalists and campaigners draw our attention to the damage that has been done and the people that have been harmed, a growing number of designers and companies are responding to these challenges with creativity and vision.

Whether we consider new manufacturing techniques that harness the power of the sun, collaborations with not-for-profit groups to develop markets and livelihoods for communities, or DIY urban food-growing systems, designers and makers are reimagining almost every aspect of our lives. Rather than tinkering at the edges of a system that needs to change, they are using their skills and positivity to redesign the system itself.

Graduate Notebook

TFRC's pick of the most exciting graduates from the BA and MA Textile courses at Central Saint Martins College Of Arts & Design and Chelsea College Of Art & Design

Hannah L Chester
Olivia Hollis
Mercy Daniels
Dahea Sun
Yuki Horie
Shamees Aden
Kate Lawson
Hiromi Itoga
Cara Marie Piazza
Azusa Dannohara
Ingrid Hulskamp
Julie Yonehara
Wiriya Techapaitoon
Susan Klara Campbell
Diana Kovacheva

Captivated

'Captivated' by Chelsea College Of Art & Design BA Textile Design graduate Hannah L Chester is constructed from reflective plastic which distorts and reflects daylight (and artificial light in the dark) plus printed fabric encased in resin. The project was inspired by the preservation properties and inherent vulnerability of ice. Hand-dyed plastics are used to create subtle shades of changing light. These futuristic reflective fabrics have not been used in a fashion context before. Hannah is currently interning for a designer while expanding her own collection; her main goal for this year is to save up for a heat press and new fabrics, as well as learn to pattern cut.

www.hannahlchester.tumblr.com
hannahlchester@hotmail.com

Hannah
L Chester

Preserve/Slice

'Preserve/Slice' by Chelsea College Of Art & Design BA Textile Design graduate Olivia Hollis takes its inspiration from the complex and unexpected cross-sections of mineral formations. Optical fibres, monofilament, strands of plastic and copper electrical wire are trapped within resin blocks which, when sliced, create an exciting alternative to bone or shell. They possess fragile qualities rarely associated with synthetic materials. The garment collection uses the relatively new process of heat-bonding plastic to plastic, requiring no stitching. Olivia is undertaking an internship at Mary Katrantzou and also sold her own pieces as part of a Chelsea graduates' collective at the Islington Contemporary Art & Design Fair, October 2012.

www.oliviahollis.tumblr.com
oliviakatehollis@gmail.com

Olivia
Hollis

Architectural Lace

mercydaniels@gmail.com

'Architectural Lace' by Central Saint Martins BA Textile Design graduate Mercy Daniels adopted an experimental process that began with drawings, continued through cutwork within paper or other relevant materials and was eventually transformed into 3D outcomes. The project sought to combine hard and soft geometric lines and the qualities of an Elizabethan ruff through the production of lace-influenced prints. A mix of laser cutting, screen prints and sublimation prints is used. Inspired by architecture, there is a repetition of structure, pattern, shape and colour that is reinterpreted through deconstruction. Mercy is currently freelancing and seeking internship opportunities and aims to build upon her techniques to produce fashion or jewellery pieces.

Mercy Daniels

www.sundahea.com
sdh0306@gmail.com

'Rain Palette' by Central Saint Martins MA Textile Futures graduate Dahea Sun features garments coloured with natural dyes that change colour in reaction to the pH levels of rainwater. Based on material exploration with red cabbage dye, samples were made combining craft skills such as knitting, embroidery and crochet. There is the potential for wearers to engage interactively, recording and uploading pH readings online to create a global database of real-time environmental data as well as raising public consciousness. Dahea wishes to develop this project further to create proof of concept, believing that visualisation of environmental impact is the key to a sustainable future.

Dahea Sun

Rain Palette

Yuki Horie

www.yukihorie.tumblr.com
yuki.0727.yuki@googlemail.com

'Pandora's Box' by Chelsea College Of Art & Design BA Textile Design graduate Yuki Horie is made from mirrored material and draws its inspiration from pop-up books and the effects of falling light. Supporting research was focused on geometric shapes and the process of an item opening up to reveal itself. Still interested in the effects of light and shadow play, Yuki hopes to develop her work by incorporating waste materials and audience interactivity.

Pandora's Box

Shamees Aden

Protocells

'Protocells: A new "living" material technology' by Central Saint Martins MA Textile Futures graduate Shamees Aden explores the potential of the emerging science of protocell to propose a future high performance trainer. The Amoeba surface-adapting trainer employs a living technology that is responsive and reconfigurable, adapting in real time to the activity of the runner by adding extra support to high impact areas. Liquid chemicals are manufactured artificially in the laboratory to form the material. Protocells could evolutionise future fabrication and product scenarios. Shamees is currently working with Protocell scientist Dr Martin M Hanczyc to fabricate a proof of concept Protocell shoe by 2030.

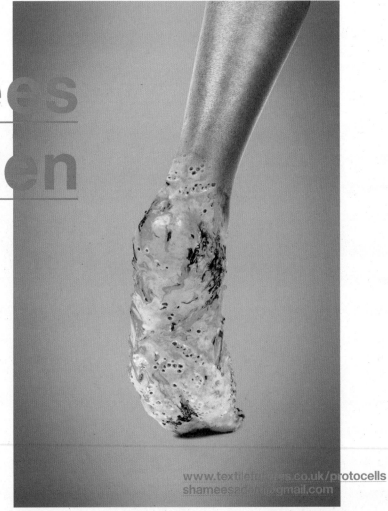

www.textilefutures.co.uk/protocells
shameesaden@gmail.com

www.katelawsontextiles.com
katelawsontextiles@gmail.com

Geometric Reflections

'Geometric Reflections' by Kate Lawson was influenced by the irregularity of reflections on London buildings, particularly the triangles of the Gherkin, and focuses on the image of a building broken down into fragments of colour and shape. The outcome was a collection of bespoke dresses displayed in front of backlit Perspex. Traditional embroidery techniques are made modern by changing the materials typically used. A new stitching technique was utilised, involving hand-dyed plastics, stitching and tessellation of shapes. Kate, a Chelsea College Of Art & Design BA Textile Design graduate, is developing the technique used in her final show into a collection of new designs as well as more commercial pieces, while gaining experience in trend forecasting and colour prediction.

Kate
Lawson

Imperfect can be Perfect

Hiromi
Itoga

itogahiromi@gmail.com

Chelsea College Of Art & Design MA Textile Design graduate Hiromi Itoga's work took the form of a series of mini-installations showing coloured glass bottles and ceramics that cast digital-print shadows onto fabric, breathing new life into the object and giving audiences a glimpse of their embodied stories. The installation of colour on fabric captures the fleeting effect of sunlight through glass, permanently recreating the original, ethereal effect. This investigation of emotional durability and value demonstrates how, through long-term use, a new narrative for objects comes to life. The immaterial and poetic is preserved and conveyed through material possessions.

Cara Marie Piazza

www.caramariepiazza.tumblr.com
piazza.caramarie@gmail.com

Cara Marie Piazza's project innovatively utilises natural matter sourced in the city. The starting point was mapping out and foraging in areas of London, inspired by nature always finding its way toward the sun despite the tarmac of an urban landscape. Each piece the Chelsea College Of Art & Design BA Textile Design graduate creates is one of a kind, made from materials found locally alongside donations from local businesses such as excess squid ink, flowers and onion skins – repurposing what would otherwise be thrown away. Cara is setting up her own studio, beginning production on her next capsule collection and working as a freelance stylist/assistant.

www.spectrumexplosion.blogspot.co.uk
azusatruck@gmail.com

Paganism

'Paganism' by Central Saint Martins BA Textile Design graduate Azusa Dannohara uses dyed sheepskin, fringes and euphoric colours to evoke the movement of ritual dance. Experimentation in dyeing processes led to the accidental discovery of how viscose yarn metamorphoses during the washing process to create a 'carpeted surface' 3D pattern, unique in something designed to be worn. E-wrapping technique was explored to achieve a tufting effect. After gaining further experience in the industry, Asuza hopes to begin a Textile MA and is currently participating with textile mentors Texprint which provides the opportunity to further develop and experiment on the project's themes.

Azusa Dannohara

'Daily Poetry – Catching a moment in time' by Central Saint Martins MA Textile Futures graduate Ingrid Hulskamp is a series of contemplative toys for adults made from blown glass. The pieces combine tactile, visual and aural experiences, counterbalancing our rushed digital lifestyle, and are open to different interactions and interpretations – just like a poem. Every part of the object is handcrafted, necessitating collaboration with skilled craftsmen to create unique objects. Ingrid is starting her own label, Daily Poetry, which will develop the principle of contemplative objects.

www.ingridhulskamp.com
ingridhulskamp@gmail.com

Ingrid Hulskamp

Daily Poetry – Catching A Moment In Time

'The Transformative Chronotype' by Central Saint Martins MA Textile Futures graduate Julie Yonehara is a collection of objects that explore the future potential of manipulating the human circadian rhythm. A luxury vanity set fits into the user's daily routine of preparing for the day and winding down at night using light and dark as stimulant and sedative. Red light spectrum signals aid rest by promoting melatonin production, while the blue spectrum signals wakefulness by blocking melatonin production. Julie has recently exhibited as part of 10 Fold Collective at the London 2012 Designers Block while establishing commissions for further projects.

The Transformative Chronotype

www.cargocollective.com/jyonehara
jyonehara@gmail.com

Julie Yonehara

basketizer@gmail.com

Chelsea College Of Art & Design MA Textile Design graduate Wiriya Techapaitoon developed a contemporary fashion collection which focused on a craft skill that is undervalued and underused in her native country of Thailand. 'Fashion Basketry' uses a simple hand-weave and plaiting technique to create garments that follow the line of the body, creating a sophisticated silhouette in a readymade woven tape. Focusing on social sustainability, Wiriya used the work to create a fair-trade production system, supporting a local workforce who learned new skills and received fair pay. Her collection was shown with a set of graphic swing tags which included information on the number of hours taken for each stage in the process of the garment's production.

Wiriya
Techapaitoon

Fashion Basketry

Susan
Klara
Campbell

'Status Update' by Central Saint Martins BA Textile Design graduate Susan Klara Campbell explores how status, value and prestige are all interwoven into society – and how traditional and modern viewpoints vary. Textiles are created by weaving established ways of showing status (medals) with current status symbols (credit cards) to form an update comprising old and new values. The fabrics are formed by hundreds of separate laser-cut neoprene pieces which have been inlaid much like a wooden table. Material used for 'luxury' – rather than 'real' – sportswear represents the idea of status being not entirely factual. Susan wants to continue to use CAD technology to develop her design work.

www.susanklaracampbell.com
susan_campbell2@hotmail.co.uk

Status Update

www.cargocollective.com/dianakovacheva
info@dianakovacheva.com

'Instinctellect: A Vocabulary Of Human Intuition' by Central Saint Martins MA Textile Futures graduate Diana Kovacheva explores our innate human interaction with objects and materials. Through a series of ethnographic workshops Diana observed and recorded our intuitive interaction with surfaces and materials, sampling a broad range of users. Analysing and editing her findings she created the ultimate handbook for designers, aiming to provide a tool to consider instinctive behaviour within the design process. Diana is publishing her 'Instinctellect' book and is now working within the Arup Foresight team.

Diana
Kovacheva

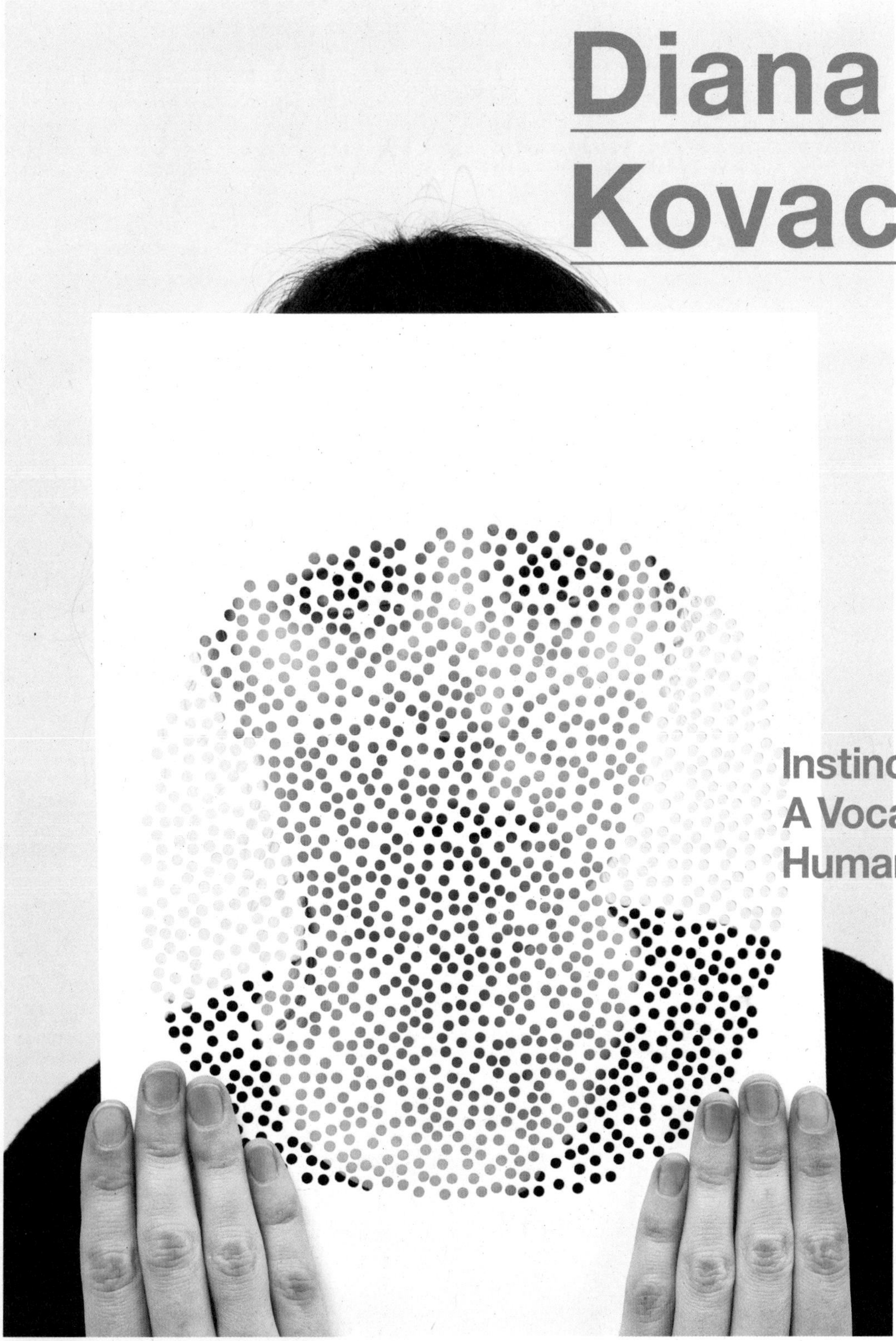

Instinctellect:
A Vocabulary Of
Human Intuition

External research funders include
Arts & Humanities Research Council (AHRC) / Technology Strategy
Board (TSB) / EDF Foundation / MISTRA and the Future Fashion
partners and collaborators / Medical Research Council / The European
Science Foundation / The European Culture Programme and our Resil-
ients partners / TED Fellowship / Arts Council England / Office Of Public
Works / Crafts Council / Craftspace / Victoria & Albert Museum /
Centre for Information Technology And Architecture (CITA) /
Royal Academy Of Fine Arts Copenhagen / Gatsby Foundation/St Johns /
East Of England Development Agency Bursary / University Of Cambridge
/ Dept Chemical Engineering & Biotechnology and Cambridge Enterprise
/ The Welding Institute (TWI) / Anglia Ruskin University / British Society
Of Perfumers / Professor Tim Jacob (Cardiff University) /
Science Technology Engineering And Mathematics (STEM) /
Research Councils United Kingdom (RCUK)

Thanks also to all our commercial funders, who include
VF Corporation / H&M / Gucci Group / Philips / The North Face /
Gainsborough Silk Weaving Studios / Sakae / Method / International
Flavours & Fragrances, Simple Essentials / Toyota / CEROMA Ltd / Slim
Barrett, Ernst & Young / International Fragrance Association (IFRA) /
Scent Marketing Institute (New York) / Hugh Parnell / Jonathan
LLoyd-Platt / Sensory Design & Technology Ltd / Marc Rolland /
John Ayres (Pandora Ltd)

Internal funders
UAL Research / the research departments at Central Saint Martins College
Of Arts And Design(CSM) and Camberwell Chelsea Wimbledon (CCW)
College Of Art And Design / Centre For Learning & Teaching In Art
& Design (CLTAD) / Creative Learning In Practice Centre For Excellence
In Teaching And Learning (CLIP/CETL) / ERASMUS programmes

With thanks to

University Of The Arts London
www.arts.ac.uk

H&M
www.hm.com

MISTRA Future Fashion
www.mistrafuturefashion.com

VF Corporation
www.vfc.com